Zagra Zephyrs
Volume One

A. A. Telmesani

Published by Tofu Ink Arts Press. All rights reserved.
Book design by Brian L. Jacobs, A.A. Telmesani, Glenn B, JLTY Atelier

Cover Image: *Siyah Mashq*, Library of Congress, African
and Middle East Division,
Near East Section Persian Manuscript Collection

Map of the Zāgra Valley by Reem Telmesani

ISBN: 978-1-958661-29-1
EPUB ISBN: 978-1-958661-30-7
www.TOFUINK.com
A member of CLMP

Āyā The Heliopolite

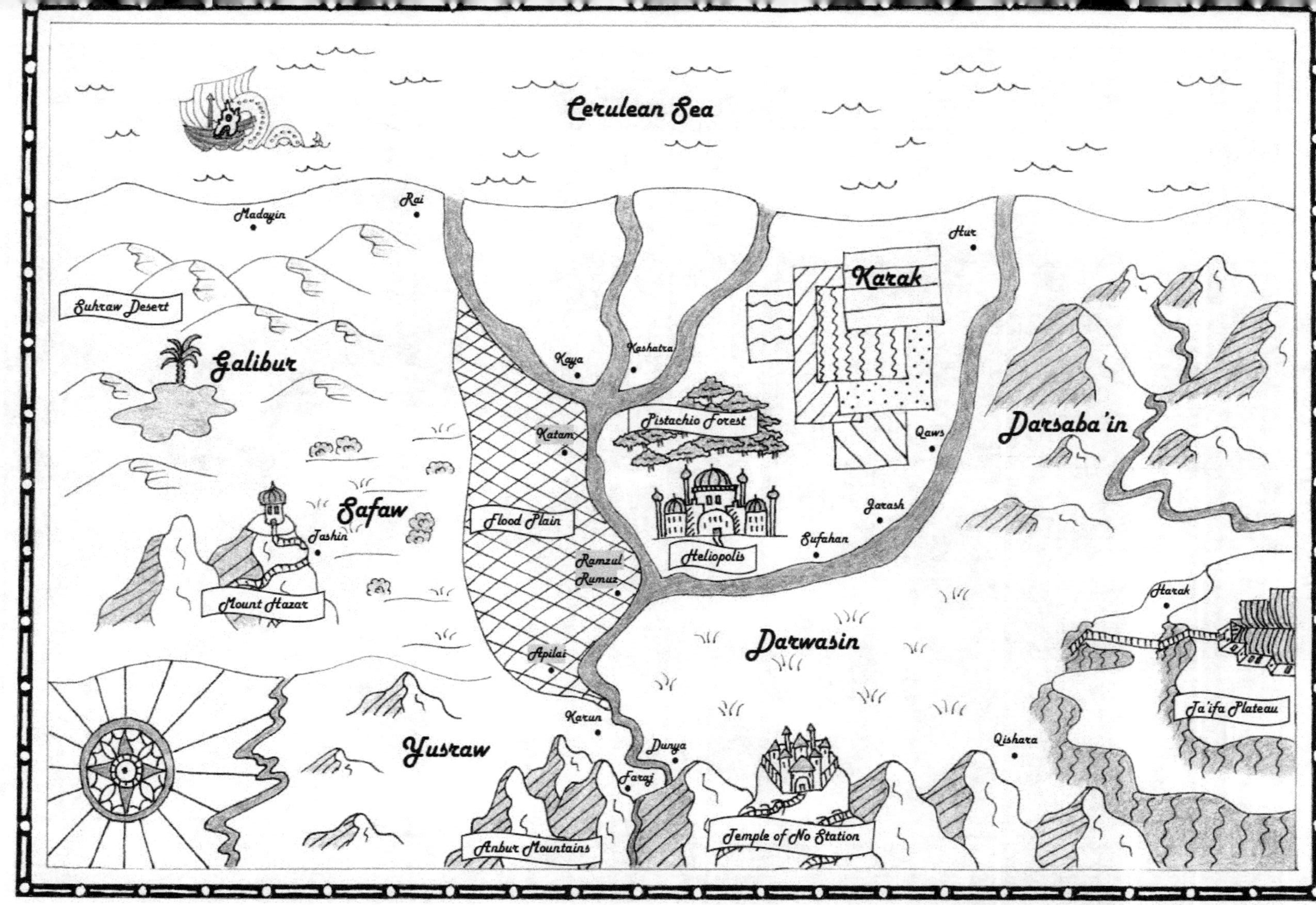

Cerulean Sea
Madayin
Rai
Hur
Suhraw Desert
Karak
Galibur
Kaya
Kashatra
Qaws
Darsaba'in
Pistachio Forest
Katam
Safaw
Flood Plain
Heliopolis
Jashin
Jarash
Sufahan
Ramzul Rumuz
Mount Hazar
Harak
Darwasin
Apilai
Ja'ifa Plateau
Karun
Qishara
Yusraw
Dunya
Faraj
Anbur Mountains
Temple of No Station

Contents

i. Preface vii

ii. Introduction 1

iii. Note on the Translation 17

I From *Metaphysics* 21
   The Alighting Place 23
   The Vast Earth of Gāiā 28
   Queen of the Clans of Fire 48
   The Isthmus 97

II From *The Blue Dīwān* 111
   Maxims 112
   Lo, in the Month of Ḏhul Qiʿdah 123

III From *Carmina Terræ* 127
   Safāw 128
   Dārwāsīn 145

IV From *Chronicles* 153
   Sanctum 154
   Sensoria 176
   Return to Ḥarak 184

Preface

It was all an accident. The creation myth was meant to be an isolated piece in a magical realist collection that would be my doctoral creative writing project. When the myth became a trilogy, I reached an inflection point that would shape the course of my literary, intellectual, and personal life forever. Once the universe had come to life, there was no forcing it back into the womb from whence it came. It immediately asserted itself, held me hostage, and compelled me to decide whether to build on it or not.

From the moment I decided to go for it, the Zāgra Valley universe truly took on a life of its own (at times, I still feel like a spectator, burdened with transcription duties). In that inflectional moment, I turned back to my master pedagogue and research subject, who sparked my interest in Sufi literature and philosophy in the first place, and who inspired me to apply for graduate programs in Islamic Studies in the spring of 2012: the twelfth/thirteenth century Andalusian mystic philosopher and poet Muḥyiddīn Ibn ʿArabī (*d.* 1240) known by his honorific title *Shaykh al-Akbar, Doctor Maximus*—the Greatest Master.

If I were to create a universe, it was to be sustained by two streams: the fount of Ibn ʿArabī and the fount of the Upanishads and Vedāntan non-dualism. The radical monist ontology and metaphysics of the Upanishads, especially as interpreted by Śaṅkara in the eighth century, share some shocking and extraordinary similarities to Ibn ʿArabī's. I refer those who wish to delve more deeply into the two schools to Reza Shah-Kazemi, who explores those commonalities at length in his *Paths to Transcendence According to Shankara, Ibn ʿArabī, and Meister Eckhart.*

My discovery of the Upanishads during the darkest days of the pandemic brought me back to life and helped me escape the oppressive throes of loneliness and homesickness. The very first page of the Br̥hadāraṇyaka Upanishad induced an instantaneous, ecstatic, epiphanic experience that qualitatively transformed me. I had experienced what Ibn ʿArabī calls a *ḥāl*, a state, a theophanic flash, a moment of Self-disclosure, a unique instant of clarity and realization of Brahmānic Oneness that affirmed the Qurʾānic Oneness of the One Real. That moment sparked a period of intense study of the Vēdas, the principal Upanishads, and Śaṅkara's non-dualist school of Vēdāntan metaphysics. These two unrelenting fountains of Śaṅkara and Ibn ʿArabī, sourced from the same well-spring, would become the primary source materials that would fuel the project for the foreseeable future.

The Zāgra Valley universe has a vertical hierarchic ontological structure. The lower stratum is the terrestrial literary landscape: an ancient river valley with the city of Heliopolis as its imperial capital. The city was built between 2107 and 2091 BCE, during the reigns of Rex Tiberus I and his son Rex Tiberus II, who oversaw its completion. The Grand Sanctuary was first constructed around an ancient banyan tree believed to be the very tree beneath which the prophetic messenger Luthayl of Rāi received her first lines of Monadic revelation. The sanctuary would become the sacred heart of the capital. Heliopolis was then built around the Grand Sanctuary. Its official completion in 2094 BCE would mark the beginning of a new Zāgran calendar—year 1 *ab urbe condita* ('from the founding of the City')

The Zāgra Valley is the categorically *physical* world of base materiality, occupied by humans, fauna, and a wide array of spirit entities and mythic creatures cursed to roam the Earth for all eternity. When spirit-consciences of human characters flee from their material bodies, whether by accident through intercession/intervention or by intentional, focused meditation, usually under the guidance of a human or spirit master, they may access the inexhaustible metaphysical spheres in the forms of celestial stations and waystations that culminate with the Station of No Station, which is the sphereless sphere of total annihilation in the divine pleroma. A distinct feature—indeed *advantage*—of metaphysical realms is the irrelevance of Time and the natural laws of physics, which govern neither space nor form; hence, *meta* physical— beyond/transcending Nature. The sphere transforms into a totally unique literary canvas without limitations—a literary realm, unburdened by the laws of physics, that challenges all preconceived notions of conventional, terrestrial literary spaces.

A famous literary example of a work that explores and exploits a hierarchic ontological structure is Dante Alighieri's (*d.* 1321) *Divine Comedy*. Each stratum in *inferno*, *purgatorio*, and *paradiso* is a distinct reality that differs qualitatively from every other stratum. The higher the stratum, the nearer it is to the beatific Reality of Beatrice. The lower the stratum, the nearer it is to the ninth circle of the *inferno*—a frozen lake that encases the treacherous. The Zāgra Valley universe operates within a similar ontological framework. Only the lowest sphere is not the ninth ring, but absolute non-existence, which is diametrically opposite to the ultimate Real, which is not just a *paradiso*, but the pure, unknowable Divine Essence, in which all that exists will be annihilated following the apocalypse—not in the fiery sense of John's Revelation, but of the original Greek apokálypsis, ἀποκάλυψις, *literally*, unveiling/ disclosure (of the Divine's ultimate eschatological plan). According to Ibn ʿArabī, nothing is farther from the Divine Essence than absolute non-existence, which makes it the true hell.

For aspiring mystics to earn access to the Station of No Station, they must purge their souls of ego—the source of all human defect— and all earthly addictions, especially materialism. The abandoning of all worldly things is the necessary first step for the aspiring wayfarer who yearns for nothing but union with Her, the Real, whose myriad Names exert their essential influences in the cosmos. The tedious daily deprecation of the ego-self must become routine.

Knowledge is Light. The ego rusts over the heart, which is a mirror. For Essential Light to reflect off the heart of a yearning mystic out into the world, they must laboriously remove the rust of ego from their heart-mirror. Through consistent burnishing, veils are lifted, which uncover steppingstones that lead to higher and higher isthmian stations. When, as spirit-consciences, wayfarers enter a station, they must discern the gnosis that that station houses. When they finally acquire the Essential Knowledge of that station, it becomes a steppingstone to the next station or waystation (a sphere with lower grades of Essential Light, but Essential nonetheless). Since it is the human spirit-conscience that journeys, all journeying is inward. The inner being becomes the doorway that circumvents both the manifest cosmos and the chaos of prime matter and leads the spirit-conscience directly to the supernal realm of Platonic Forms. Through focused meditation and divine favor, the mystic can plunge into the imaginal realm of the isthmus—the in-between, the strip of land that separates two seas, i.e. the corporeal realm from the ethereal realm of spirits.

In the Zāgra Valley universe, there is an infinite number of stations that together house the sum-totality of all cosmic Knowledge. There are therefore infinite ways to journey towards the Real, and each station provides its own facet of Essential Knowledge that the wayfarer accumulates as they ascend to Her along the cosmic chain of being. The acquisition of varying degrees of gnosis provides them with a limitless variety of Essential Knowledge, making the wayfarers unique receptacles and diffusers of gnostic Light. And the beneficiaries of that Essential Light, as a reward, receive a unique Name or Quality of the Real—one of Her Self-disclosing traces discerned by the receptive gnostic. For each Letter of the native Zāgran Kūfic script, there is a station. A Name combines the Knowledge of the individual Letters that form them. The stations of the Names are Her most beautiful abodes. Therefore, the stations of the sacred Letters and Names are superior in nobility to all other stations save those of the Numbers, with the numbers 'one' and 'no-number' as sovereigns that rule over all other numbers. They command the same dignity and obeisance as the Names. The sacred Names and Numbers respectively represent the Platonic and the Pythagorean cosmological aspects of the Zāgra Valley universe. Pure Forms, pure Numbers, same cosmos.

Essentially, Knowledge is everything to the aspiring wayfarer. It is Knowledge that dispels all ignorance in the corporeal world. Knowledge lifts veils that obscure the next stepstones up the chain of being. Crucially, Knowledge must be *recognized*, for we contain the multitudes—the totality of all Divine Knowledge—within the confines of our being, specifically, according to Ibn ʿArabī, the heart. The sacred saying (*ḥadīth qudsī*, extra-Qurʾānic revelation revealed exclusively to the Prophet Muḥammad) that Ibn ʿArabī and other Sufis continuously reference regarding the heart as the only receptacle capable of containing the Real proclaims that "Neither My Earth nor My Heavens could contain Me, whilst the heart of My believing servant does contain Me." It is, therefore, a matter of journeying inward, purging the ego, and recognizing the latent Knowledge within us. Attachment to the material blunts our discerning faculties, and the rust of ego prevents all Essential Light from shining through.

In short, Knowledge is the key to union with the Beloved. Through wandering, good works, continuous remembrance of the Names, and the recognition of Her manifest signs across the two horizons, the wayfarer earns divine favor and is rewarded with the gnosis required to ascend the heavenly stations toward the Station of No Station, where all is annihilated in perfect union with the One.

The mystic paths that Yāsīn, our poet Āyā the Heliopolite, and her fellow disciples pursued would have entailed indefinite wayfaring (i.e. roaming the terrestrial and celestial realms, embarking on a simultaneous outward and inward journey toward the Beloved), constant, unrelenting meditation on the Names, Attributes and the Oneness of Being, performing supererogatory deeds and selflessly serving the communities of the Zāgra Valley. All the extant written records they produced along their journeys make up the vast majority of the Anbūr Codex Collection. This present collection is a small anthology of Āyā's poems from various longer works that exist *in potentia*. An in-depth survey of Āyā, her life and times, school of thought, literary corpus and its critical reception is provided in the fictional introduction immediately following this preface.

Finally, I would like to express how indebted I am to so many people, without whom this whole project could and would not have been possible, beginning with my mother and father, who've supported me throughout my personal, academic, and professional journeys, allowing me to pursue my artistic endeavors that collectively culminate with this publication; to my sister Reem, who has always had my back, no matter what, and who also produced the stunning map of the Zāgra Valley included in this book; to Lynne, who took me in during a trying period in my life, who was patient enough to listen to me reciting cantos to her over coffee, bacon and eggs, and in whose house I truly became a poet; to Max, John, Peter, Ned, Lily, Sam, Majd, Brian, Cadi, and John Goodby for helping me through the darkest period of my life, when I was stranded on a remote isle across the pond, pursuing a PhD that, from its inception, exactly coincided with the Covid-19 pandemic; to Dr. Ruqayya Khan, who taught me more than I deserve, who provided me with the intellectual foundations I needed to pursue my creative explorations and with the hermeneutical tools I continue to use in my research of Sufi literature and philosophy. Without her, this collection categorically could not have materialized.

I especially wish to express my love and appreciation for my supervisor at Swansea University, Dr. Alan Bilton, who shepherded me through the entire PhD/Covid pandemic, keeping me sane, alive, and writing every day during the darkest periods of deep depression and homesickness, and whose supervision facilitated the creation of this literary universe. This project is the most important thing in my life. It is my singular *raison d'être*. Without Alan, the Zāgra Valley would have remained a nonexistent entity. I cannot, nor do I wish to imagine a life without it.

Finally, I want to express my love and appreciation for my late friend Chris Cornwell, who I miss dearly, who unlocked and inspired the poet in me, and who changed my life in so many subtle and substantial ways from the very moment we met to the night I left South Wales for good seven years later. I treasure every moment we had together. He was a human and a poet of the highest order, and the reason I went back to Wales in 2019, because I knew he'd be there. I dedicate this collection to him.

A. A. T.
November 2025
Turners Falls, MA

==== Fiction enters here ====

Introduction

The 1963 cache of 598 vellum codices discovered during an excavation of the Gāian Temple of No Station in the southern Anbūr Mountains led by Hermann Liebewicz' team of archaeologists from Emerich University remains one of the most significant archeological finds of the 20th century. The sacking of Heliopolis by the Tarkanids in 983 BCE (766 *auc*) was a unique historiographical catastrophe in which the written records of an entire civilization were nearly wiped out in three calamitous days of carnage. The Dār al-Ḥikma Library and her three to five million vellum codices and papyri scrolls were either burned in the fire that destroyed the great library, or tossed into the Zāgra River, along with the bodies of Heliopolites that the Tarkanids slaughtered mercilessly during the total sacking of the capital. Literary works of prose belles-lettres, heroic epic and lyric poetry, scientific manuals, philosophic and mystical treatises and tractates, official histories, hagiographies, heresiologies, bureaucratic records, and the like, were irretrievably lost. This is what makes the discovery of the 1963 Anbūr cache so important and extraordinary. It is simultaneously the largest, oldest, and most intact body of extant Kūfic literature. Prior to this discovery, the only surviving works of Zāgran literature were short treatises, dawāwīn, historical records, and fragments of Greek and Coptic translations of the original Old Kūfic texts.

The diverse range of literature—diverse in form, genre, category, and function—reflects the diverse preoccupations of Zāgran literary and philosophical figures. Their fascination with creative literary forms is unique among other pre-classical civilizations, with unparalleled production of major and minor works of prose, poetry, and plays. The general character of the writing could be considered sacred in nature, though lacking the fiery dogma characteristic of similar genres of writing *de jour*. Secular multi-genre works make up a small portion of found Kūfic writings, and typically take the form of isolated fables, legends, and pastoral poetry.

Although these authors habitually signed and dated their manuscripts, a substantial portion of the canon remains anonymous. Moreover, one must account for the prevalence of misattributions, forgeries, and plagiarisms—deceptions that were ubiquitous throughout the classical and pre-classical eras. Roughly 71% of the codices in the collection are signed and/or dated by their authors and are considered by Gustav Hitz to be "correctly attributed beyond a reasonable doubt." (Hitz 24) What is enormously helpful is the fact that close to 90% of the 598 codices seem to be a single library belonging to a specific Gāian sect, led by a cult figure and his followers. The adherence of the philosophical and ascetic gnostic views espoused in these writings to a singular Gāian school of metaphysics—that of the Prophet Yāsīn (d. 1070 BCE) and his disciples—lends a surprising sense of intellectual and theological coherence to the material. The most significant of the anonymous texts is the *Creation Trilogy*. These codices are—with respect to timbre and register—complete outliers among all extant Kūfic works of the classical period. The *Trilogy* presents a novel retelling of the genesis story found in the Cylopiad, the sacred scripture of the Gāian religion indigenous to the Zāgra Valley. The theory that Yāsīn and his disciples authored these anonymous works is contentious, but, crucially, the philosophical views of the *Creation Trilogy* are remarkably consistent with Yāsīn's school of thought. Scholars and readers are free to draw their own conclusions. What is salient to us with regards to the author of this present collection is the fact that Āyā the Heliopolite (*d.* 1060 BCE), along with Sākina (*d.* 1063 BCE) and Huthayfa (*d.* 1080 BCE) the self-abdicated king of Kārūn, were Yāsīn's most intimate and principal disciples. Therefore, it is necessary to understand Āyā's brand of metaphysics within the context of Yāsīn's broader cosmological framework: a generally monistic cosmology rooted in the Self-disclosure of the Real—the unique deity of nearly every Zāgran religious sect—who discloses Herself within the cosmos in the form of traces of Her panoply of divine Names and Attributes, which are identical to Plato's perfect Forms.

Translations of the Yāsīn codices by scholars at the Jivāna Institute of Kūfic Studies are ongoing. Religion and Philosophy departments across the world eagerly await the opportunity for Yāsīn's mystical non-dualist philosophy to become an integral part of the discourse and be contextualized alongside other monistic schools extant in the region between the thirteenth and ninth centuries BCE.

An in-depth examination of Yāsīn's fundamental philosophical principles is regrettably beyond the scope of this publication, which is a small anthology of poems written by Āyā the Heliopolite—an extraordinary woman and mystic philosopher who became a great master in her own right and guided many wayfarers along the path— both human and jinn. This is merely the first of many batches of English translations of works from her prodigious corpus, which makes up roughly a third of the entire 1963 Anbūr Codex Collection.

I hold the distinct honor of being the curator of the entire Anbūr Codex Collection at Emerich University. The mission—dare I say *calling*—of our interdisciplinary team of scholars at the Jivāna Institute is to catalogue and translate the entire codex collection systematically. The length of time the project will take is irrelevant. That we have this body at all is a blessing and a boon to humanity and to the budding field of Kūfic Studies. Prior to the discovery of the 1963 Anbūr codices, our primary sources for the study of Zāgran socio-political history were limited to surviving fragments from the heresiologies of theologians like Quintanius (*d.* 687 BCE), Dominic (*d.* 541 BCE), and Titus of Qaws (*d.* 313 BCE), as well as the extant portions of Sharajād's *Histories* (*d.* ~ 995 BCE). The *Histories*, by scholarly consensus, remains one of the most authoritative primary sources by an ancient Zāgran historian, who thankfully wrote his annals less than 300 years after the death of our poet. Raya Hazm, a fellow at the Jivāna Institute, has published a critical translation that will remain of utmost importance to modern historiographers of the region for decades. Her commentary on nearly every line in the recension is invaluable (and I am happy to report that a critical study of Hazm's commentaries by Thomas Frank of Claritas University is in the final stages of pre-publication). It is, therefore, astonishing to find historical works by unofficial (i.e. popular) sources that paint a more coherent and complete tapestry of Zāgran history. These texts represent the socio-political perspective of the populace—everyday people from the Yusrāw to Dārsabaʿīn. They were recorded by humanist wayfarers who cared more about others than themselves; being immovably apolitical, they theoretically had no reason to show favor to any particular group. Partisanship was anathema to Yāsīn and his disciples.

Thanks to the Anbūr codices and the highly literate mystic philosophers and poets who wandered the Zāgra as neutral, unaffiliated observers who transcribed their journeys and produced highly original creative and philosophical works along the way, our knowledge of Zāgran socio-political history has increased dramatically. The translation of these codices will be a daunting, but necessary task. It will be a major collaborative effort conducted by specialists at universities and institutes across the globe, but one that will reveal a rich historical tapestry and shed brilliant light on an ancient civilization that has languished in relative darkness for centuries—such was the devastation of the violent upheavals and sackings of Heliopolis and its libraries. This is to say nothing about one of the most devastating natural disasters in human history: the eruption of Mount Kresos on the Cerulean island of Tirax, which blanketed the entire delta and spelled the final doom for Heliopolis. It was an event that would make the eruption of Mount Vesuvius in 79 CE seem like a bad weather day.

The Life and Times of Āyā the Heliopolite

Āyā (1134-1060 BCE), a born and raised Heliopolite, witnessed the extraordinary horrors of the genocidal conflicts that marred the late Ġhufrānid dynastic age. She endured the brutal reigns of Ġhufrān IX (who declared himself Dictator in perpetuum fifteen years before Āyā was born) and Ġhufrān X, whose overthrow and execution by the Yusrāwan Barābara during the sacking of Heliopolis in 1105 BCE brought an end to the dynasty.

The biographical data that Āyā artfully weaves into much of her poetry affirms that she was of humble origin. Her father, Hāshimī, and mother, Zulaykẖā, were multi-generational tanners and leatherworkers of modest means. The strategic location of Heliopolis (nestled precisely where the Zāgra and East Zāgra Rivers split) almost immediately turned the city into the hub of all commercial activities in the valley, allowing easy access for merchant ships and caravans year-round. Despite this bustling commerce, the strictures of the two-person operation meant that Hāshimī would spend several months out of the year tanning, dyeing, and curing hides. During those months, Zulaykẖā would run the dukkān in the central bazaar, where she crafted and sold leatherware. As soon as Āyā was old enough—as early as five years old, by her own estimation—she began crafting products and assisting her mother in the dukkān. Though this eased Zulaykẖā's burden, the family business never really prospered. The premature death of Hāshimī in 1119 BCE was a multifold tragedy for the family. Zulaykẖā, suddenly a widow and single mother, was left to assume all business duties: the tanning, the curing, the weaving of goods, all while simultaneously running the dukkān in the bazaar daily. It was simply too much for her and Āyā to handle, and the family business folded immediately.

That year would prove monumental for Āyā personally. First came her chance discovery of a group of mystics in the Sanctuary during one of her habitual nightly escapes. It was there that she met her first true master, a woman named Sukayna, whom the reader encounters in the poem "Sanctum." This was followed by her discovery of Yāsīn and Huthayfa, the death of her father, the collapse of the family business, her forced engagement to Minas of Dāmarkand, its violent repercussions, and her permanent departure from home to become a full-time devotee. Unfortunately, the start of her mission under the Ḥarakite's guidance first required deliverance from a trial of epic proportions. In "Queen of the Clans of Fire"—a long poem selected from her multi-volume opus *Metaphysics*—Āyā recalls the vivid and gruesome details of the harrowing ordeal that befell her within weeks of joining the ranks of Yāsīn and his novitiates. To avoid spoiling the narrative, I defer to Āyā to recount the event herself in the poem, which I have rendered in unrhymed pentameter.

Following the death of Yāsīn in 1070 BCE, many of his long-time disciples went their separate ways. Some continued wayfaring like Āyā and Sukayna (*d.* 1063 BCE), while others retired, choosing a more sedentary life, or reintegrating into their old communities. Over nearly a quarter-century of wandering the Valley with Sukayna, Āyā's literary output was prolific, encompassing volumes of lyric and epic poems as well as prose works, including the philosophical treatises in *Metaphysics, The Life of Yāsīn,* and *The Life of Sukayna.* In the latter work, Āyā chronicles her wayfaring with Sukayna through the corporeal and subtle realms, noting that rarely were they alone. Āyā claims that she and Sukayna were always accompanied by Ḥasākīn—the shape-shifting jinn who serves as her guide in the poem "Queen of the Clans of Fire"—the malāk, or archangel Elia, whom Āyā inherited from Yāsīn after his passing, as well as other transient entities of light and smokeless fire who joined them at various stages of their journeying.

As of this publication, there are no available critical editions or full translations of any of her prose works. Thankfully, the coordinated efforts of specialists from across the globe to translate and produce critical editions of the Āyā codices are promising indeed. I regret that this short introduction does not allow for a detailed sketch of Āyā's extraordinary life as a saint, poet, and wandering master, for she is the stuff of legend, a mythic mystic, and the heroine of her own epic. I invite readers interested in learning more about Āyā's life and school of thought to read the comprehensive and authoritative biography *Axial Saint: The Life and Way of Āyā the Heliopolite* by the brilliant Marwa Shaheen, Chair of the Kūfic Studies Department at Corinth College.

Āyā's Corpus

The Āyā codices represent roughly 35% of the Anbūr Codex Collection. The conservative number of codices attributable to her is 209. Most are short philosophical treatises and belles-lettres (118) that do not exceed a few dozen pages. Twelve are hagiographies of saints like her life-companions Sākina and Yāsīn, his mother Roā the Messenger, Leāna the Hermit of Ḥarak, Bayān of Rāi, Waraqa, and six other prophets from across the Zāgra Valley. The remaining seventy-nine codices comprise various dawāwīn of poetry, poetic prose, dramatic poems, and philosophical poems, as well as her poetic magnum opus, the epic *Kitāb al-Manāzil* (Book of Spheres).

Āyā's dawāwīn (sing. dīwān, collection of poetry) exhibit her vast knowledge of Kūfic grammar and prosody, as well as her mastery of all thirty-two traditional *buḥūr* (stanzaic forms; sing. *baḥr*, lit. sea/ocean) of Zāgran poetry. She also introduces invented *buḥūr* of her own, which radically break from tradition, both prosodically and thematically. Her mastery of poetic genres is also evident. Āyā composed odes, or *qasāʾid*—long, foundational, polythematic poems, often 100 lines or longer, with a single complex meter, brutal monorhyme throughout, and a tripartite structure (the amatory prelude (*nasīb*), the journey description (*raḥīl*), and main purpose (*madīḥ*); fragments or *qiṭaʿ*— shorter, more flexible, often monothematic poems focused on a single event or idea; popular or vernacular *rajaz*, composed in a specific meter, used for didactic or descriptive purposes that aim to push the lexico-graphical limits; strophic poetry or *zajal* composed in dialectal Kūfic; and *rubāʿī*, or quatrains, both rhymed and unrhymed, composed of stress-based lines that range from tetrameter to heptameter. The most prominent themes in her poetry include panegyric (*madīḥ*), satire (*hijāʾ*), elegy (*rithāʾ*), love poetry (*ghazal*), wine poetry (*khamriyyah*), ascetic poetry (*zuhdiyyah*), and purely descriptive poetry (*wasf*)— characterized by descriptions of Nature, flora, fauna, battle scenes, major events, and ekphrastic descriptions of art and architecture.

Āyā's magnificent celestial epic *Kitāb al-Manāzil* (Book of Spheres) describes her ascension through the isthmian spheres and stations along her journey to the ultimate abode of the Real. Each stratum up the ontological chain presents a major trial that Āyā must overcome to acquire the essential Knowledge to proceed to the next stratum of her ascension through the spheres. The style is heroic epic of a high vernacular, and the meter is a fluid dactylic pentameter (*mutaqārib*, "approximating" or "harmonious" meter). It is Āyā's mystical *summa*. It is as much an encyclopedia of esoteric knowledge as it is a supernatural, psycho-spiritual *bildungsroman* of epic proportions.

Through remarkable unrhymed dactylic pentameter, Āyā peels away the veils that dim the Light of essential Knowledge and refracts its beams directly toward the reader. The Jivāna Institute and Emmerich University have commissioned me to produce a critical English translation of the *Kitāb al-Manāzil*, which has occupied the last six years of my life. It is a distinct privilege to be producing the first ever English translation of the *Manāzil*. Throughout the process, I have been in regular consultation with my colleague at the institute, the brilliant Chloé Milou, who is preparing the first ever French translation of the epic.

Extraordinarily, Āyā also claims that fourteen codices, though written by her hand beyond a reasonable doubt, were not original compositions, but books authored by Yāsīn. She asserts that he dictated them to her nightly, line by line, via the imaginal isthmus from his prison cell in Heliopolis, where he spent the last ten years of his life. She begins these works with a doxology and a prologue in which she identifies herself as a "transcriber of wondrous things," crediting the Ḥarakite prophet as the sole author of the codices. In *Life of Yasin*, she recalls how

> Time does not govern the isthmus, nor does space delimit it. He was as free in that prison cell as we were in the fig grove [of the Ḥarak monastery in the western Tāʾifā]. This was his opinion, not ours.… Sākina and I spent the better half of each day out of body, beyond the veil that separated the worlds. In the isthmus, we resumed all prior practices of meditation, recitation, prayer and contemplation of the mysteries. We learned that, for these practices, the physical body was a surplus requirement. Late into the night, and with increased frequency in his final years, Yāsīn was able to complete his unfinished dawāwīn, tracts and treatises by reciting every line to me, which I transcribed verbatim. Facilitating this was the great honor of my life. I never felt closer to him.

Yāsīn's *Maqāmāt* (Book of Stations)—transcribed visions of celestial stations in which he awakens while entranced in meditation, recounting his experiences in those realms and the essential Knowledge acquired following a trial—is perhaps the most notable and creative of the fourteen codices that Āyā claims Yāsīn dictated to her during his decade of imprisonment until his death. Final philosophical testaments, works of prose and poetic parables and maxims, a long contemplation on the Names, and other treatises make up the remaining dictated codices. These additions to the twenty-six other graphologically verifiable codices attributable to Yāsīn would see his extant corpus expand to forty works.

The only other work that Āyā claims was dictated to her from the isthmus was a book of contemplations (*Kitāb al-Ta'ammulāt*) by none other than Yāsīn's mother, Roā the messenger, daughter of the Kashāṭran house of Boutamīm. According to Āyā in *Life of Yāsīn*, Roā was in her early teens when she died shortly after giving birth to Yāsīn, who was miraculously conceived. In *Life of Yāsīn*, Āyā describes how Roā woke up one morning at dawn to find herself fully pregnant up to term, when the day before, she was "like a slender reed plucked from the Zāgra":

> The angel descended upon the slumbering sandal-bearer and met Roā's ethereal Self on the shores of the isthmus that separates the corporeal and subtle spheres of divine imagination. The child awakened in the imaginal plane and was awed by the sight of Elia, who appeared to Roā in the form of a child of Gāiā. The disguised angel offered a bowl of milk to the girl, who did not hesitate in consuming the draft. As she returned the bowl to Elia, Roā began to feel faint and drowsy. The angel laid her down gently in her lap until she fell asleep, then transported her back to the corporeal plane.
>
> Roā awoke around daybreak curled up in agony on the cold stone ground of her living quarters, clutching her belly, which, by some unknown alchemy, had expanded alarmingly overnight. Feeling the bulge of her belly, Roā was utterly confused, utterly frightened and ashamed all at once.

Having lived such a short corporeal life, Roā's *Kitāb al-Ta'ammulāt* seems even more extraordinary, as she dictates to Āyā—in a formal literary register beyond the capacities of a typical twelve to fourteen-year-old child—her contemplations of tribal conflicts in the delta that marred her short life in retrospect as a spirit-conscience. Roā had posthumously accompanied Yāsīn, Āyā, and Sākina as a spirit-conscience for over two decades by the time she dictated her *Ta'ammulāt* to Āyā line by line from the isthmian realm. Appended to Roā's *Ta'ammulāt* is a short genealogy of prophets and messengers who she claims she met there. Later in life, Yāsīn would significantly expand on his mother's prophetological appendix in his sacred genealogy *Kitāb al-Anbiyā'* (Book of Prophets).

Milieu

Simply put, Āyā's recently discovered cache of seventy-nine poetic works changes the landscape of Zāgran literary history and scholarship. Though her corpus only further cements the 11th-10th centuries BCE as the golden age of Zāgran poetry. The milieu in which she flourished included an extraordinary pantheon of male and female poets, whose works are largely lost to us. The few dozen dawāwīn we do have from them are invaluable, and there is a concerted effort to produce critical editions and translations of each codex. It is worth noting that the yield of discovered codices from current excavations is promising indeed, and I suspect we will recover more works from that great assembly of poetic luminaries. Of course, time will tell.

Arguably the greatest poet of Āyā's age was another Heliopolite: the heroic epic poet Bilqīs (*d.* 1127 BCE), whose *Kitāb al-Mulūk wal-Malikāt* (Book of Kings and Queens) is the ancient predecessor to Ferdowsi's (*d.* 1020-1026 CE) epic the *Shānameh*, a work roughly one fifth the length of its Kūfic ancestor. Bilqīs' epic chronicles the mythical and historical past of the Heliopolite empire from the Monadic Creation up to the reign of Ġhufrān IX. It includes, but is not limited to, tales of monarchs and their houses' histories, conflicts, legendary heroes, and epic battles. It is considered a masterpiece of world literature and is a cornerstone of Zāgran language and culture which cements Bilqīs' status as one of the greatest poets of all time.

While Bilqīs' epic is an exoteric mythopoeic chronicle of earthly monarchs, Āyā's *Manāzil* by contrast is an esoteric chronicle of an inward journey of metaphysical ascension up the isthmian chain of spheres. Both epics characterize the distinct lives of the two poets who composed them. Bilqīs came into the orbit of Ġhufrān IX through Ḥarb (*d.* 1089 BCE), a trusted advisor of the Paterōn and generous patron of the arts. Bilqīs' relationship with Ḥarb obligated her in turn to support the Paterōn's political and social reforms. *Kitāb al-Mulūk wal-Malikāt* helped Ġhufrān IX restore a sense of national pride and traditional Zāgran values like virtue, duty (to deity, family, and country), and piety, all of which the Paterōn was actively promoting. *Kitāb al-Mulūk wal-Malikāt* became the national epic of the Zāgra Valley and the literary crowned jewel of the House of Ġhufrān.

As discussed at length in previous sections, Āyā's early wayfaring career required the abandoning of all earthly things as the first step of an aspiring wayfarer's journey. She practiced a simultaneous inward and outward journey, transcribing her travels and visions along the way. While Bilqīs justifiably enjoyed the diverse fruits of her labors, and of her exalted status as the imperial poet-laureate of Heliopolis, Āyā strove to serve the communities of the Zāgra Valley while smothering and snuffing out the ego that craves recognition and acclaim. Nonetheless, Āyā's and Bilqīs' thematically polar poetic contributions place them both in an exclusive stratosphere of their own. They represent the two towering pillars that support the proud edifice of Heliopolite poetry. It is a shame Bilqīs did not live long enough to read the masterpieces of her eternal rival. The great poet died when Āyā was only seven years old.

Other notable poets of the age include the likes of Māya of Azra Kāf (*d.* 1190 BCE), a physician of the body and the soul, whose allegorical masterpiece the *Tuyūrān* describes her own inward journey to the Real, and was a major influence on Zāgran mystic poets ever since. Her principal disciple and mystic poet Hind (*d.* 1086) whose spiritual development was profoundly transformed by her meeting with her master, guide, and travel companion. Both were as renowned for their wayfaring as they were for their prodigious literary production. Hind is best known for her twelve-volume dīwān of mystical quatrains, the *Ilāhiyyāt* (Book of First Philosophy) chronicling her esoteric and exoteric wayfaring. The last major poet of the age was the mystic philosopher and poet Ṭarafa of Tāshīn (*d.* 1066 BCE), whose highly complex and influential system centers on the doctrines of the Names and the Oneness of Existence. His works of metaphysics justifiably overshadow his poetic corpus, which is unfortunate, as his nine-volume *Buḥūr al-Raḥmān* (The Seas of the Compassionate) for centuries remained one of the most popular and widely read dawāwīn across the Zāgra Valley. We know that copies of the *Buḥūr* were available at every library and academy in the Valley, not to mention the records of the grammarians of the age, who agreed on nothing, but were unanimous in their love and veneration for the encyclopedic poet.

Reception

Perhaps the greatest mortal danger Āyā faced in her life was persecution by Rex Paterōn Ġhufrān X, whose theologians roundly condemned her "subversive and impious" literature, which by her late twenties was already in wide circulation. Consequently, Āyā, Sākina, and their disciples were forced into hiding for seven years. However, their lifestyle as an ever-wandering group of wayfarers made them difficult to track. Furthermore, they were beloved by the people in the communities they served, who gladly aided and abetted their evasion of imperial eyes. It is hard to overstate how beloved Āyā was throughout the Valley. Besides the people whose lives she touched and the communities she served, thousands of her poems in which she champions the people and popular reform (or "insurrection" in the eyes of the Paterōn) were set to music and sung across the Valley for generations. It took the intercession of a trusted wazīr to the Paterōn to finally end the valley-wide manhunt: Faras Ibn Nūr (*d.* 1105 BCE). He was a man of letters who harbored sympathies for Gāian mystics, born of his admiration for Āyā᾽s dawāwīn.

Her most influential detractor was the theologian and virulent heresiologist Bin Tuwayma (*d.* 1067 BCE). He belonged to the Benāwid school, known for advocating a strict, literalist interpretation of Monadic revelation and for rejecting what he viewed as "obscene deviation" from the tradition. His accusations of blasphemy against Āyā focused on a few key doctrinal points. Bin Tuwayma strongly opposed Āyā᾽s concept of Oneness, which he misinterpreted as blurring the distinction between Creator and creation, leading to the grave heresy of pantheism. He vehemently condemned Āyā᾽s doctrine of the Names and Attributes, finding her interpretations to be grossly allegorical and heretical deviations from their literal meanings.

> Her method of interpreting the Names and Attributes involves allegorical displacement of the plain meaning. This is a clear heresy. Since these interpretations are unsupported by canonical texts, the true significance of their essence is effectively nullified.

Bin Tuwayma also rejected the idea of the Real's indwelling in Creation and the concept of mystical union with the Divine. He found the notion to be highly blasphemous. To him, it fundamentally contradicted the Cylopiadic tenet of the Real's transcendence and distinctiveness from Her Creation.

> The tenet that the Creator and the created are coextensive and non-distinct is a theologically abhorrent notion and an explicit rejection of faith. The persistent ambiguity in their discourse on the divine and the mundane posits that the cosmos is identical to the Deity, and vice versa. Such a stance constitutes clear pantheism, a doctrine that stands in direct opposition to our Monadic tradition, and a clear heresy.

Other tenets Bin Tuwayma vehemently opposed included Āyā᾽s doctrines of Gāia᾽s genesis and her Vast Earth, the Seal of Sainthood, and the authority of revelation versus mystical intuition. Despite the rumor that he enjoyed Āyā᾽s wildly popular mystical poetry, his fanatical rejection of her core beliefs, coupled with fiery public excoriations from the grand pulpit of the Sanctuary, played a material role in Ġhufrān X's inquisition and ultimate persecution of her and her followers.

Later in life, Āyā would enjoy the safety and security of her imperial patron, Rex Waratha I, who idolized her. He had grown up reading her dawāwīn, singing her songs, and mimicking her poetic style in his youthful compositions. In 1075 BCE, she obliged Waratha's request for an audience. The young Paterōn was so impressed and awed by the elderly Gāian master philosopher-poet that he asked—rather than commanded—that she instruct him in the philosophical and poetical sciences. Uncharacteristically, Āyā obliged the Paterōn, taking a two-year hiatus from wayfaring to remain in Heliopolis to instruct him. Naturally, his sponsorship further increased the circulation of her poetry. By the time Waratha made her Poet Laureate of Heliopolis in 1067 BCE (the year Bin Tuwayma died), her dawāwīn graced the shelves of nearly every home and the stacks of every library and academy in the Zāgra. This achievement, witnessed within her own lifetime, was matched only by the great Bilqīs, who had died before Āyā had even written her first poem.

The Poems

This book is a small anthology of poems that I have chosen from four separate dawāwīn, which collectively represent a variety of genres and are written in various traditional and innovative forms. It is meant to be a bite-sized sampler of her diverse poetic oeuvre and an entryway into her dazzling ontological multiverse. I have intentionally excluded the predominantly philosophical dawāwīn from the pool of candidates, as I believe the prose treatise to be the superior vehicle for Āyā's philosophical discourse. To be clear, her collections of philosophical poetry are masterworks and deserve to be treated as such. However, they tend to be brutalist, cerebral, even acrobatic at times, bordering on the absurd.

The first major challenge was choosing from a dizzying myriad of genres that represent her broad poetic corpus. What first impressions were I to give a modern reader of Āyā and her poetry? After a period of contemplation and consultation, I settled on the following:

Part I consists of four selections from her multi-volume *ilāhīyāt*, or *Metaphysics*. "The Alighting Place" is a poem that delves into the nature of the waypoints that mark the wayfarer's inward journey and ascent up the ontological chain toward the Divine Pleroma. These waypoints represent successive levels of insight, metamorphosis, and experience. The chain of alighting places serves as the celestial highway—the metaphysical medium for astral wayfaring and the means of acquiring Essential Knowledge, or gnosis. In the poem, Āyā provides an expansive definition and examination of the esoteric facets of these alighting places and their sacred origins.

By contrast, "The Vast Earth of Gāiā" is a cosmic creation myth in verse that describes the birthing of the cosmos, the arrangement of its hierarchic structure, the genesis of prime matter, and the terraforming of Gāiā's Vast Earth. The creation myth unfolds unrelentingly; the reader is swept along with the poem's swift-winged protagonist, who journeys under the aegis of the Real through whom Creation blooms via the primordial stations of the sacred Letters. It is also an account of the creation of diverse entities of light and smokeless fire, and of the demiurges charged with forging existence from the quantum foam of non-existence. Following "The Vast Earth of Gāiā," is one of the longest poem in the anthology—the aforementioned "Queen of the Clans of Fire," a description of her isthmian journey through a jinn temple on an astral plane. In the poem, Āyā is introduced by her jinn guide Ḥasākīn to Queen Āshturumāzda, who the mystic poet entertains with revealed insight and tales of earthly trials. I have chosen to render the poem in Miltonic unrhymed pentameter, which conveys an approximate sense of the original unrhymed, stress-based pentametric lines.

Part I concludes with a poem on the nature of the imaginal isthmus and its essential qualities. The term *barzakh* literally translates to "isthmus," "barrier," or "partition." In Yāsīn's cosmology, the *barzakh* is the barrier between sweet and salty water that prevents them from mixing—an analogy for the separating membrane between the subtle and the phenomenal. It is the demarcation between shadow and light. The *barzakh* is also known as the imaginal world, or the world of (hanging) images. Pure meaning (i.e. spirits) can assume form in the isthmus and be perceived by human spirit-consciences.

Through practice, meditation, guidance, and grace, human mystics can freely access, actively participate in, and exert their influence within the imaginal isthmus. By contrast, the rest of humanity accesses the isthmus passively when dreaming, and permanently upon death, where their spirit-consciences will abide until the Gathering Cry (i.e. the Real's eschatological unveiling).

Part II is a pair of poems from Āyā's *Blue Dīwān*: a compilation of fifty maxims, and an ode in dedication to the One Reality ("Lo, In the Month of Dul Qiʿda") which I have rendered in the same loose dactylic hexameter as the original Kūfic composition. It was a dangerous choice, but conveying a sense of the original meter made it seem worthwhile.

Part III is a selection of two poems from Āyā's *Aghānil Arḍ* (*Carmina Terræ*, "Song of the Land") which celebrate the diverse regions of the Zāgra Valley and the multi-ethnic communities that inhabit them. *Aghānil Arḍ* can be viewed as the predecessor to Virgil's *Eclogues*. Both of Āyā's poems in this section are selected fragments from longer pastoral poems that celebrate the regions of Safāw in the central valley and the highlands of Dārwāsīn north of the Tāʾifa.

Part IV rounds out the anthology with three autobiographical/self-reflective poems that chronicle episodes of Āyā's terrestrial life. The first poem "Sanctum" is a recollection of a traumatic event that she experienced as a child prior to meeting Yāsīn and Huthayfa. "Sensoria" is a classical ode detailing a minor existential crisis that Āyā went through in her early adolescence. It is a raw emotional expression of grief and a cry for answers regarding the realities of things as they truly are. The poem culminates with a fiery statement of defiance that expresses a desperate wish for ego-death. And finally, in "Return to Ḥarak," Āyā describes her two-year sojourn at the Ḥarak monastery high up on the Tāʾifa Plateau, where Yāsīn and her fellow companions sought refuge following the traumatic events described in "Queen of the Clans of Fire."

Note on the Translation

My philosophical approach to translation, especially of ancient Kūfic, adheres to the technique championed by the Secretary of Foreign Tongues and translator Bin Ḥunayn (*d.* 873 CE), as lauded by the grammarian Marakān of Rāi (*d.* 921 CE). This method of *sensum de sensu* (meaning-for-meaning), involves ascertaining the full meaning of a whole sentence and expressing it in the target language with an identical meaning, rather than relying on the inferior *verbum de verbo* (word-for-word) technique of matching individual words. Following this method, I aimed to produce an accessible English text for a broad, modern readership, consciously avoiding an English riddled with transliterated Kūfic terms that would estrange the reader.

While a translator's first drafts often lean toward the literal *verbum de verbo*, the final, accessible quality is achieved through rigorous revision and rehearsal with objective eyes, i.e. uninfluenced by the original Kūfic syntax. This allows the translation to be scrubbed of infelicities and replaced with a more lucid, modern version that faithfully conveys both the author's message and their original tone and register. This process, which does not release the translator from the obligation of detailed linguistic knowledge, promises a greater hope that the work will be accessible to a wider audience. Paradoxically, adopting a modern English register makes it easier for the reader to comfortably inhabit the world of Āyā's ancient poetry.

Any inadequacies, obfuscations, or failings are mine alone and were entirely unintentional. I am no "interpreter of wondrous things," but a humble servant with the honest though impossible task of translating and transmitting Āyā's extraordinary treasury of mystical poetry to a modern, global Anglophone readership. The weighty responsibility of the task is an omnipresent specter that haunts me nightly. However, if reading Āyā's poetry induces a fleeting theophanic moment of clarity in but a single reader, I will consider my efforts vindicated.

Richard Dubreuil
Horus Hawkley Professor Emeritus of Kūfic Studies
Department of Philosophy & Religion
Emmerich University

Do not compete with anything
other than a chameleon,

for it resembles the state of existence
and the aroma of its musk is lovely.

Ibn ʿArabī
Bulāq Dīwān
CDLXXI

Part I
From *Metaphysics*
Kitāb al-Ilāhiyyāt

The Alighting Place

And coursing the vast, unfolding spheres
of emanation, the folk of divine descent
on wingèd beasts unveil in subtle code
the stations of lunar bodies, the gaseous orbs,
and the twelve sublime zodiacal towers.

Theirs is the promise of the alighting place
that awaits them at their journey's end.

≈≈≈≈≈≈≈≈

Through corridors of stations and abodes
they fly, each realm increasing in degree
of nobility and proximity to the Throne,
towards the presence of the beginningless
and all-encompassing Determiner.

The station of no-station is their reserve
along with the keys to Her vast treasuries.

≈≈≈≈≈≈≈≈

Nocturnal meeting houses bear insignia
above the entryways that indicate
which Letter, Name, and Cylopiadic Sign
their zāwiyā adheres to faithfully.

The ones who verify and recognize
the signs and ciphers of the Gatherer
inherit Her bounties and drink directly from
the generous well-springs that brim and flow
with the rich elixir that every gnostic craves.

They say 'Remember me in your refuge,
for no-one recognizes Her but Her.'

≈≈≈≈≈≈≈

In the book of Time and Consequence, She says:
'Shall no-one recognize My visage, or know
the measure of My account concerning the Truth
or know the reason why I come to My own
at night through traces and manifestations of Me?'

'O Night! See how My signs are visible
across the two horizons and etched upon
the palpitating hearts of humankind.

Remember Me in your seclusion, friend.
Recite from Mine, the divine Cylopiad.
Recite from the plethora of psalm
and verse therein. Transmit them interest-free.

Serve those who yearn for Me a wine unmixed
and do not settle for a lesser blend.'

≈≈≈≈≈≈≈

And She also said, 'Let Me disclose
to you, O servant of the Compassionate,
the secrets of the cosmos most sublime.

Delight in the Word of your Clement Advocate.
Do not come to Me in the solitude
of night for intercession on your behalf
or on behalf of others close to you
when in your heart a malignant seed takes root
and rust diminishes its pristine gloss.

For I will recite My book in a dialect
familiar to you. Verily, it is your own!

Allow Me to be the ear with which you hear,
the eyes with which you see, the tongue
with which you taste, for you are the folk
of divine tasting, and yours is the sweetest wine;

the hand with which you touch and feel,
the feet with which you go and then
come back to Me, your granter of security.'

≈≈≈≈≈≈≈≈

'Am I not your Lord, the Beginningless
Establisher of Ways? And when I ask,
'Which of My portents do you deny?'
you feign stupidity and ignorance
when in your heart you are aware of Me,
for truly I am the heart within your heart
and so, I know the secrets kept therein.

I am the Unmoved Mover of celestial Forms,
The First Cause, the Active Intellect,
the Preserved Tablet and all that emanates
from My dominion, descending
   from sphere to sphere.

If you consider yourself among the folk
of that alighting place, then I have chosen you
and taught you the courtesies particular
to your bloodline of saints and messengers
and made you fit to join their noble ranks.'

Thus spoke the Eternal Reality,
and She is the Merciful Inheritor
of lunar and sublunar bodies that move
by Her free will and follow unerringly
their sound, pre-calculated courses.

A. A. Telmesani

≈≈≈≈≈≈≈≈

Interpreters who live to differentiate
between the states, stations and their degrees
of proximity to the majesty of Her abode
approximate their days and nights away
fixated—yoked by their own intellect,
when other faculties disposed to them
are better suited to apprehending Her.

Their eyes are fixed on the finger pointing to
the moon, not on the comely moon itself.

≈≈≈≈≈≈≈≈

The guarded treasuries of the guiding lights
extracted from the depths of beginningless
eternity contain vague traces of code
that would perplex and vex the intellect
attempting to decipher the mysteries
of nonexistence in a world of Forms.

The most discerning among the Māshawites
would waste away attempting to ascertain
the subtle metaphysics pertaining to them.

Avoid the hypocrites
    with newly starched habits.

        Ours are coarse and well-worn
compared to theirs from years of wayfaring
and roaming the lunar and sublunar planes
across the vistas of Gāiā's Vast Earth
and up the chain of celestial stations.

≈≈≈≈≈≈≈≈

Perform ablutions and upraise yourself.
Pursue the station of *kāf* and the guiding lights.

The axial luminaries of your epoch
are masters of gnosis stripped of sensorial
and imaginal data that contaminates
the unrestricted in-rushes of Self-
disclosure from behind the subtle veil.

Their vintage is as pure as any kind
and pressed from a fruit of sacred origin,
found neither in the East nor in the West,
selected from an inverted mother tree
whose ancient, penetrating roots run deep
    into the oversaturated soil
of Gāiā's resting place in that Vast Earth
of pure hyle, unmolded and uncured.

≈≈≈≈≈≈≈≈

The people of the alighting place perceive
what She reveals to them of Her facets
and qualities made manifest upon
the two horizons and etched upon their hearts
that fluctuate, wherein the Truth will be
unveiled, and we will recognize that She
is the Real through whom Creation occurs,
the hand that moves, the Benignant Gatherer,
the Afflicter and the Bringer of Reckoning.

And when She makes Her traces manifest
in the world of ensouled beings and on
the isthmian shores that demarcate
the realms of jinn, corporeal creatures
    and subtle entities,

the gnostic will recognize the alighting place
and ascertain the seventy thousand mysteries
of every guiding light that led her there.

The Vast Earth of Gāiā

I

In the wake of the Great Becoming
when the First Intellect descended
the spheres from its sublime dominion
and met its receptive cosmogenic mate—
the preserved tablet of prime matter
mud—the Vast Earth came to be.

It was fashioned and fixed in its place
within the hierarchy of the Fashioner
and held the most esteemed station
among the earliest of created things.

From its mud is fashioned all that is
possible, for the Vast Earth is literally
the imaginal domain of the third eye,
where the potentiality of every entified
existent is either formed or left unfulfilled.

For untold eons the Vast Earth reigned
supreme among all existent entities
until the dawn of manifestation unveiled
the orbs and the solar and lunar bodies
that burned ferociously for whole epochs,
then began to cool and eventually harden.

And the constellations were also set,
with each designated its own station
in the vast dome of Her dark empyrean.

This increasingly controlled and ordered chaos
eventually produced the ideal conditions
for the Fashioner to gather Her mud
and fashion firm land to support living things.

At that nascent cosmogonic stage,
the entire cosmos, which included
these newly formed lunar and sublunar
bodies, as well as the expanding æther
in which they burned, fit comfortably
     within a mustard seed.

And when the appointed hour arrived,
the Fashioner took that mustard seed
and sowed it in the fertile soil of absolute
     nothingness,
as far from the throne
     of the unknowable Essence
          as possible.

When the time came some million
eons later, which measures to one
millionth of a moment for the Fashioner,
a shoot shot out from the absolute
darkness of non-existence that shone
from the billions of gaseous bodies
condensed under extreme pressure
within the mustard seed that germinated
and released its shoots of rarefied light
and lit the nothingness, and spread
outward, sending its gaseous couriers
along their pre-calculated courses
bearing news that there is no reality
other than the Real, the Unmoved
Mover who moves the astral bodies
and who established the hierarchies
in the chaos of beginningless eternity.

And when the Fashioner disclosed
Her maternal secret to creation
and breathed of Her Essence
into the cosmos, the moisture
from Her Breath brought life
to the burnt-out gaseous entities.

Yet there was one extinguished orb
that the Fashioner seemed to favor
over other orbs;
               and She engulfed it
with the remaining primordial waters
from the almighty life-giving Breath.

And for a million more eons that orb
remained encompassed by the waters
until the appointed time the orbits
of fourteen suns and seven moons
were fixed upon precalculated courses
in the empyreal dome;
                   and the days
and nights became brother and sister,
and between them equilibrium reigned.

The chosen orb engulfed in the primordial
waters baked in the heat of the fourteen
suns and cooled beneath the seven moons
that shifted the tides of the firmament
until the first spot of dry land appeared
that was so miniscule, it would be invisible
to the naked eye in the age of Seeing.

The Fashioner then took that minute plot
of soil, saturated with every nutrient,
and stretched it out in all directions.
And the dry terrain advanced against
the receding tide, but it too ran

its precalculated course and ceased,
and the Vast Earth gained sovereignty
over her domain from shore to shore.

Then the Fashioner disclosed Herself
as an ancient seed, and the demiurges
sowed the ancient seed in the nutrient-
rich mica-speckled Vast Earth mud.

But after an inestimable number of eons,
not one shoot shot out from the mud,

      when *ex nihilo* the Fashioner
disclosed Herself as a great rain cloud
that split open and emptied its contents,
and down came the primordial waters
that activated the Vast Earth mud
and caused the seed sown in the pit
of pre-eternity to germinate at last.

     Truly, Vast Earth mud
       is of a peculiar kind.

≈≈≈≈≈≈≈≈

The first primordial tree to ever grow
in any ontological domain or station,
long before the age of living beings,
was an inverted tree whose boughs
and branches grew deep underground
and whose fruit fertilized its own plot
and produced thick, burgeoning roots
that broke the surface of the rich soil.

The roots knotted and curled together
over a span of seven thousand life cycles
until a novel form began to manifest.

Then the first ever instance of violent
fracture took place when this gnarled,
novel form broke from its mother tree.

The Fashioner then took this fallen debris
and fashioned it into a most beautiful form.

≈≈≈≈≈≈≈≈

When Gāiā awoke from her preternatural
slumber, she found that sacred instrument—
the Creator's calamus—lying there beside her.

And just as the Aleph enabled the Letters
and liberated them from the wombs
of their fixed, pre-eternal lunar mansions,
the calamus enabled newborn Gāiā
to liberate all potentiality from its state
of dormancy—of absolute non-existence.

All that is doomed to that pitiable state
is a matter sublime and the unique reserve
of the Real through whom creation occurs.

≈≈≈≈≈≈≈≈

If the Throne of the Sovereign, and everything
encircling it, and the Footstool and the fountains
and the mellifluous streams and rivers of Firdaws
and the totality of existence that birthed existence
and the Garden, the Fire and all that they contain
were gathered up into one conglomerate and placed
beside the Vast Earth, it would be like comparing
a single grain of sand to mighty Mount Anbūr.

But in that grain were strange and wondrous things
whose metrics can in no wise be discerned,
measured or fathomed by the human intellect.

With every life-giving Breath,
the Real creates within Her Vast Earth

    worlds within worlds
        that spawn and multiply.

Even the utter void of sukūn cannot
envelop her, so sublime and vast is her
presence among the first created things.

    II

The gnostic who enters the Vast Earth
after being struck by an inrushing flash
of Self-disclosure abides in this domain
for a mere instant—barely long enough
for their eyes to feast on the pleroma
of archetypes in their purest forms.

But only the prophets and messengers
possess free license to enter and leave
by their own volition at any time.

≈≈≈≈≈≈≈≈

For the aspiring wayfarer, the road
to sainthood is long and littered
with the snares of everyday life
that tether her to material things.

There is no material key for the lock
on the door of the ambrosial wine-cellar.

The wayfarer must wander the vistas
of corporeality indefinitely to prepare
herself for the infinitely more difficult
and perilous inward ontological journey
from one station to the next, acquiring

and actualizing her mystical contents
along the long arc of her cosmic ascent,
incessantly knocking on the door of gnosis
until the Keeper of the Garden mercifully
unlocks the door to Her fathomless domain
and offers her a drink from Her own cup.

It is a joyous day when the Keeper grants
access to Her vast domain of essential Forms.

III

The demiurgic powers were tasked
with stretching out the left-over clay
from the High Throne to the Footstool,
from sukūn to the twenty-eighth Letter,
the measure of which is known only
to the sublime Fashioner, who knows
all that is hidden and all that is manifest
in Her creation,
                    when one of the powers,
weighed down by their prescriptions,
questioned the Fashioner's cosmogony.

Such was the generosity of the Fashioner
that She combined speech and sight
for the sake of the blighted demiurge,
who spoke from the primordial pulpit,
saying, 'O Sovereign, will you not unveil
the contents of Your vast treasuries
and populate these fecund territories
with animate beings to roam its vistas?'

The Fashioner then seized the demiurge
and fashioned it into self-cognizing
creatures that mingled and multiplied,

and from the left-over matter nourished
the plane with every mineral nutrient.

From this action, the demiurgic powers
came to know Nature's first principle
and the realities of things as they truly are.

≈≈≈≈≈≈≈≈

When another demiurgic power spoke out,
the Fashioner this time fashioned out of them
strange entities that soon would interpenetrate
the full strata of veils that would split the spheres.

The rich prime matter that was the second
rebellious demiurgic power yielded genera
of existents that occupied their own realms;
and out of Her own goodness, the Fashioner
bestowed on them the gift of metamorphosis.

And the pleromata of demiurgic powers
dispersed the tidings of the Prime Mover
and saturated the Vast Earth with creations
of wondrous origination, and armies
of entities of flesh, fire, clay and water
populated the vast terrain of the third eye,
filling the æther with news of their origins,
for every non-delimited existent is a trace
of a Name among names that name the one
Named who is the divine origin of all names.

IV

In the age of the Great Tribulation
between the tribes of flesh, fire, clay
and water that spanned multiple
eternities without beginning or end,

the membranes between the spheres
grew porous, and incisions became
slits that turned to tears that turned
    to yawning chasms.

The entities interpenetrated freely
with expansionist zeal as they tired
of their boundaries and grew covetous.

There were the dæmonic creatures
of subtle essence—the shiqq, the ʿifrīt,
the marīḍ, the nasnās and the qarīn—
all of whom shrunk at the sheer sight
of beings of pure light—the malāʾika.

Among the dæmons were insubordinates
entirely ignorant of their true status
in the hierarchic chain of being.

They sought to challenge the malāʾika
who, in turn, utterly annihilated them.

In this humbling display of humiliation
and consequence, the beings of fire
came to know their ontological place,
and with humility prostrated themselves
in the presence of the sublime malāʾika,
favored among subtle beings by the Alive,
the Real through whom creation occurs.

Halted at the highest sphere, the beings
turned to one another, formed alliances
and began the first existential scourge.

The realms below the Footstool suddenly became
infested with the jānn of Jahannam—impure jinn
    admixtures destined for the Fire
        of ultimate nonbeing—

who were dissatisfied with destroying their own
    kin of smokeless fire, and inflamed
      with desire for the spheres
that up to this point had sealed them out.

But it was the noble jinn who penetrated
    the subtle veils of the sphere
of the descending Letters, whose stations,
like outposts, overlooked the vast domain
of the Fashioner, and marked the stepstones
of the First Intellect's maiden enterprise—
      not them.

The rapacious conglomerate of jānn
were laid low at the very first station—
the station of *hamza*, of the Highest Pen,
uniquely created by the All-Encompassing
for the First Intellect without intermediaries.

Only one creature, in this nascent reality,
was granted full permission to traverse
the entire hierarchic structure of the cosmos:
the winged Burāq, who bore the standard
and wore the ensign of the First Intellect.

≈≈≈≈≈≈≈≈

Burāq sped through the station of *hamza*
and was anointed by the Highest Pen
before being welcomed at the entryway
of the station of *hā'*, the Universal Soul,
the Upraiser and the Preserved Tablet.

In her fineries, the Universal Soul praised
Burāq and disclosed news of her own
genesis as the first upraised creation.

She then revealed the prototypes of all
cosmic activity, receptivity and polarity,
and the swift-winged being came to know
the nature of things as they truly are,
and Burāq was entrusted with knowledge
of every trace denoting every attribute
emanating from the Monadic godhead.

Burāq then pierced the next barzakh
and entered the third station of ʿayn—
Nonmanifest Nature in eternal obscurity—
hidden yet manifest in the four qualities
that exercise Nature's ruling properties
over everything in the vast cosmic ocean
save Her own parents—the Soul and Intellect.

Burāq then crossed the next barzakh
and entered the sacred station of ḥāʾ—
the vast treasuries of the First Hyle,
the storehouse of clay prime matter.

The swift-winged being marveled
at the demiurgic powers as each one
under the Merciful's aegis fashioned
one form after another, filling the void
with the subtle underlying substance
of all Creation, of light and dark matter
tracing back to the names 'the Manifest,'
'the First' and 'the Last.' Thus did Burāq
come to know the ciphers of this sphere
and its ancient decree: all things arise
from the Last and return to the First.

≈≈≈≈≈≈≈≈

Burāq then penetrated the next barzakh
and entered the sacred station of ġhayn,

the sanguine body of fertile Gāiā,
the All-Body and faculty of the Fashioner.

The swift-winged emissary witnessed
the wondrous creation of corporeality
in totality—all that will be *in potentia*
and all that will return to the storehouse
when the Creator gathers Her creation.

To Gāiā belongs all material substance.
Her dominion is density and subtlety.
Only she is blessed with the sensoria
to navigate the firmament freely
without the need of sign or cipher,
for she is her Creator's greatest Sign.

≈≈≈≈≈≈≈

In the station of *khā'*, the noble Burāq
entered the sphere of the All-Forming
where the swift-winged being witnessed
the next exquisite phase of manifestation
following the amorphous and uniform
corporeality of the station of the All-Body.

In this sphere, all existent bodily things
in the nascent universe became distinct
from one another, and the name the Wise
ruled over them, putting each in its place
and determining their appropriate forms.

In the guise of eternity without beginning,
each form praises the name 'the Formless'
and longs to return to the ocean primordial
of the Real through whom creation occurs.

≈≈≈≈≈≈≈

Burāq then penetrated the station of *zāf*—
the Throne of the All-Encompassing Real,
made known to us in the divine Cylopiad
in the far distant age of sensorial beings
upon which the All-Merciful Reality sits
and encompasses the manifest universe,
including the realm of pure imagination.

Burāq then crossed into the station of *kāf*
where the noble being witnessed the first
imaginal thing within the all-encompassing
embrace of the Throne of the All-Merciful.

It is the station of the Footstool, ruled over
by the name 'the Possessor of the Final Hour'
and the precise locus where the Real let down
Her two feet—one mercy, the other wrath.

Above the Footstool, nothing exists but mercy
and yet it embraces the totality of existence
in the lower spheres of divine emanation.

At the feet of the Footstool, the prescriptive
command annunciates our cosmic origins.

It is by the signs and ciphers of the Names
that we may recognize where we came from.

≈≈≈≈≈≈≈≈

Burāq then crossed into the celestial spheres—
the starless sphere, the sphere of the fixed stars,
and those marked by the orbits of the seven
visible orbs—the Sun, Jupiter, Mars, Saturn,
Mercury, Venus and the suspended moons.

In the station of *jīm* the winged one witnessed
the black satin sphere ruled by the name

'the Seeing'; the starless sphere that manifests
the visible entities of unspecified celestial orbs
and bodies that designate the lower realms.

These are the twelve-towered constellations—
the storehouses of the sublime nonmanifest.

≈≈≈≈≈≈≈≈

In the station of *shīn*, swift-winged Burāq
was dazzled by the sphere of the fixed stars,
within which the luminous hylic reservoirs
praised the name that ruled their properties—
'the Determiner,' who determined the Letters
to be unleashed from their primordial mansions
by Aleph under the aegis of the single Monad.

These waters dictated the interactions between
the twelve zodiacal towers and the waystations
that together drove their constant movements
and mutations in the spheres of lower degree.

Fleet-winged Burāq then flew from one station
to the next: through *yā'*, the first heaven, ruled
by the name 'the Sovereign' and its associate,
Saturn, and the spirit of the prophetic heritage;
through *ḍāḍḍ* and the ancient name 'the Knowing,'
associated with Jupiter and the line of Safadiān,

through *lām*, the third heaven, ruled by the name
'the Subjugator,' who subjugated the planet Mars
and drew the ineffable spirit of the line of Yathrib,

through *nūn*, the fourth heaven, ruled by the name
'the Light,' that bears the Sun's brilliant standard
as will the prophetic lines of Qaws and Ishfān
when they greet the hordes at the calamitous Hour,

through *rā*, the fifth heaven, ruled by the name
'the Form-Giver' and the spirit of the line of Jurjān,

through *tā*, the sixth heaven, ruled by the name
'the Enumerator,' whose creed dictates the course
of Mercury and the blessed lineage of Jabellāwī,

through *dāl* and the closest heaven, 'the Clarifier,'
whose orb is the moon, whose spirit is Yāshūwaʿ—
the one who spoke in ciphers with the Sovereign—

when winged Burāq at last entered the spheres
of the elemental globes and the station of *ṭāʾ*—
fire—ruled by the name 'the Restorer'; *zāʾ*, air,
ruled by the name 'the Alive'; *sīn*, water, 'Life-Giver,'
and *ṣādd*, Earth, 'Death-Bringer.'

                                Noble Burāq
then met its progeny, *ẓāʾ*, the minerals, 'the Sure'—
thāʾ, the plants, ruled by the name 'the Provider,'
and *dhāl*, the animals, and the name 'the Abaser.'

When noble Burāq reached the realm of spirits,
the winged being was greeted by jinn emissaries
from every house, along with their retinue,
and ranks of luminous malāʾika, distinguished solely
because they are forged from light, while jinn
are purely beings of smokeless fire—closest
in configuration to the human form; for both
are conscious subjects, prone to forgetting,
compelled by the prescriptive command
   of the Highest Pen.

Each clan of smokeless fire belongs to the station
of *fāʾ*, and are ruled by the name 'the Fortifier,'
whereas the clans of light belong to *bāʾ*, 'the Subtle,'
for they are the All-Merciful's subtlest creations.

≈≈≈≈≈≈≈

Having witnessed the blindingly radiant malāʾika,
whose unique prime matter is the light of gnosis,
and having greeted each clan of smokeless fire,
Burāq then pierced the infinitely subtle isthmian veil
separating the spheres of the spirits and the spheres
of humankind—that perfectly imperfect creation—
that being of clay sublimely fashioned by the hands
of the All-Merciful, Most Compassionate Gatherer.

At the station of *mīm*, Burāq met the matriarch
of every messenger, saint, and prophet in the age
of the fiery kiln, all of whom would become pariahs
accused of heresy and cast out of their native lands.

Burāq prostrated before the matriarch of prophets
and she returned a gesture in acknowledgement
of the noblest of wingèd beings ever formed.

The matriarch then parted the subtle isthmus
and ushered Burāq into that wondrous station
wherein the wingèd being met the unbroken
chain of prophets, saints and messengers,
not in the flesh, for that is the stuff of Vast
Earth mud, but as eternal consciences—
their unique essential spirits most sublime.

In the language of archetypes—that ciphered
Cylopiadic code—the eternally conscious spirit
of each prophet, saint and messenger informed
Burāq of their imminent Earth-bound missions.

They fed swift-winged Burāq pure manna—
gnosis of the highest order—and the wisdom
inherent in the name 'the All-Comprehensive.'

Therein are vast libraries that house multitudes
indecipherable to all but those who joyously
forfeit their will to that of the Unmoved Mover
and take utmost pleasure in being contingent
secondaries of the nondelimited First Cause.

≈≈≈≈≈≈≈≈

And Burāq came to know the name that ruled
the station of *qāf*: the name 'the Supreme,'
the macrocosmic name of the divine Essence
bestowed to humankind from the very first
moment the First Intellect and World Soul
found one another on the eve of pre-eternity.

The act of investing beings of clay with the key
to the treasuries of the All-Comprehensive
and the vast reservoirs of knowledge therein
would drive the malā'ika and clans of fire,
consumed by envy, to the brink of annihilation.

Their demise is the realization that humankind
possesses the sum totalities and they do not.

≈≈≈≈≈≈≈≈

The prophets were generous with Burāq
and offered the being their brimming chalices,
and the creature consumed their offerings
and was overwhelmed by an awesome vision
of the name 'the All-Encompassing,' gathering
all the Names and configuring human beings,
fashioning them into loci of Self-disclosure
for they are the all-encompassing engendered
thing, the proprietors of the Names and lakes
of liquid light—those reservoirs of knowledge—
and the essence of the tablets of the Cylopiad.

The matriarch invested in Burāq the creed
of humankind and the promise of their return,
then guided the swift-winged being through
the twenty-eighth and final isthmian veil
and into the station of *wāw* and the name
'the Uplifter of Degrees' that ruled the Sun
within the sphere of Gāiā's vast domain.

The Uplifter raises in degrees who She wills
and diminishes whomsoever She desires.

She is the All-Compassionate Mercifier
who entrusts the all-comprehensiveness
of Her essential Being within the womb
in the form of Her panoply of Names.

≈≈≈≈≈≈≈≈

At birth, all of humankind shall suffer
the plague of forgetting and the scourges
of insatiable greed and contagious pride.

The perfected unborn being shall forfeit
her treasuries of archetypal knowledge
at birth and spend her life recovering
all the primordial Names that preserved
her perfection within the womb.

By knowing the cosmos, we come to know
the microcosm. By knowing the microcosm
we come to know the Alive's essential nature.

And just as the cosmos has infinite degrees
in its unfolding, the Uplifter of Degrees
unfolds human existence in the form
of a flesh-bound journey of vicissitudes.

Each moment of individual existence
is a waystation on the path of returning.

≈≈≈≈≈≈≈≈

Without exception, no one entered the final station
of *wāw* without evidencing perfect knowledge
of the Letters and the Monadic mysteries therein.

And when probed by the demiurgic powers,
the wingèd being in the language of archetypes
began to extoll the qualities of the first twenty-seven
pre-eternal mansions of sacred Letters in detail,
describing precisely their subtle topologies,
leaving nothing out, exposing every crevice
with a seemingly impudent effortlessness

when suddenly Burāq fell mute at a critical point
    in the narration of its cosmogonic voyage.

The matriarch then whispered in Burāq's ear
the final code to unlock *wāw*'s storehouses,
and the keystone of the panoply of Letters
was set in its place and the mansion's gates
burst open, and with the force of ten thousand
waterfalls the dams that contained the lakes
of liquid light were felled, and the waters
of gnosis washed over the eminent Burāq
and gilded its wings with ambrosial mail
and removed the rust-like cosmic residue
from its journeying through the twenty-seven
preceding stations.

                    When the reservoirs
of light emptied themselves, they revealed
a wondrous, redolent garden ripe with fruit
of every kind, wild with mellifluous streams

and meandering rivers of milk and honey,
and the full host of prophets, messengers
and saints reclining on plush purple dīvāns,
reciting sumptuous odes and epic poems,
recounting their genesis and the tragedies
of their corporeal futures in the fiery kiln.

And Burāq lost all sense of time. Eons flew by
during which the wingèd being consumed
vast quantities of prophecies and portents
from axial saints and messengers regarding
the pre-ordained ordeals of their communities
while eating manna, quaffing unmixed wine
and rejoicing in eternity without beginning or end
when a flash of Self-disclosure struck Burāq
in a tremendous moment of divine clarity,

and the wingèd being acknowledged the Signs
of Gāiā's wondrous preternatural domain,
and with the blessing of the demiurgic powers
was given license to freely roam the hierarchies
under the unique aegis of the Granter of Security
until the calamitous Hour of the gathering Cry
splits the heavens and rends the edifice asunder.

Queen of the Clans of Fire

While taking rest along the merchant's route
through Zāgra's floodplains south of Āpilāi,
I slipped into sukūn's most sacred plane
beyond the infinitely subtle veil
that separates the realms of humankind
from those of non-corporeal entities.

Around me concrete structures seemed to hum
a frequency inapprehensible
to human faculties sensorial
and seemed to radiate a mystic glow.

These indicated unequivocally
that I was in a realm imaginal.

I contemplated my unique confines
and realized that I was in a crypt
of some jinn temple in a distant sphere.

The only seeping source of light inside
this dark concourse was ornate oil lamps
that burned blue flames of sacred origin.
In front of me loomed giant double doors
engraved in code I'd never seen before.
Above my head were vaults of honeycomb
design with splendid calligraphic script
that ornamented brilliant tesseræ —
each one a variant shade of rich azure
arranged in patterns so impossible,
whole armies of humanity's expert
geometers would forfeit their own craft
to spare them from embarrassment and shame.

I planted my left shoulder to the doors
and heaved; they dragged against the temple floor,
resisting, fighting me for every inch.
I left that crypt and stepped into a hall —
a vast memorial to the jinnī clans.

Around five hundred houses of esteem
were represented, forged of precious ore
directly sourced from Gāiā's sprawling Earth.
Emblazoned proudly on the chiefs' breastplates
were crests that glowed an amaranthine hue.

I stopped to scrutinize a few. I ran
my fingertips across the artfully
embossed house crests. I made a vain attempt
at reading labyrinthine hieroglyphs
familiar to the beings of fire alone
and by the Real through whom creation blooms.

I tried committing some to memory
to meditate on them another time.
Perhaps I'd find a representative
somewhere within this dream-state citadel
with knowledge of the houses' histories.

The blue eternal flames emitting from
the oil lamps imbued the dim concourse
with a diaphanous, æthereal tinge.
They flickered as I passed, as if to warn
the chiefs of all the clans of my trespass.

The silence in that hall was so profound,
each flicker sounded like a cracking whip.
The more I focused on the dancing fire,
the more afraid and anxious I became.
I wondered whether I was being tried
for perpetrating some egregious act
on Earth that merited a reckoning.

The creaking hinges of some distant doors
disturbed the deathly silence, startling me.
A rushing wind blew through the corridor
that caused the flames to flicker and to flare.
I trained my eyes upon the dark abyss
that was the end of this infernal hall
that kept receding, ebbing constantly
away, when in the distance I observed
a blue-flamed lamp held high.

                    I strained my eyes
but was unable to make out the form
of what was wielding it. I feebly cried
'Hello?' to that mysterious entity
without receiving a response in kind.

To my alarm, no footsteps touched the floor
beneath the movement of the floating lamp.
My heavy tread re-echoed like a bell.
I grit my teeth, picked up my feet and ran
toward the being! when in a flash the jinn
shape-shifted and revealed its noble form—
æthereal, subtle, vaguely humanoid,
configured, forged and fashioned out of fire
that burned without emitting smoke at all,
that swirled beneath the flowing hooded frock
that well-concealed its luminous visage.
Beneath the hood, its red and gold aspect
bore incandescent, piercing eyes that burned
with that severe blue flame of paradise.

'O ancient kin to humankind, I come
in peace! Do tell, what is this sacred space?
What sphere within our Maker's hierarchy
does this sepulchral sanctum occupy?'

The tremor in my voice was plain to hear
despite the growing feeling of increased
security around this temperate jinn.

'Hello, Āyā, my dear,' the jinn replied,
'We've been expecting you for quite a while,
eons, in fact—would you believe? Now come,
the hostess of this citadel will be
well pleased to hear that you've arrived at last.'

That voice! I know I've heard it in the past,
in that Vast Earth—the sound of Gāiā's voice,
or that of one of her rare seed who've roamed
our mortal plane since pre-eternity.

'Kind friend, if I may ask, what is your name,
and what is your particular employ
in this mysterious isthmian abode?'

Without turning to me or slowing down,
the gentle jinn eventually replied:

'My dear Āyā, do you not recognize
my voice? Surely the years flown by have not
diminished your capacious memory,
for I've known you of old and you of me.
Was I not there when you ascended to
that bounteous domain of Gāiā's Earth?
Or when I met you at the gates of Qāf
before you faced the hordes of infidels
that cursed the name of the Compassionate
and threatened you with stones and enmity?
Or when I greeted you on Mount Hazar
the day they laid the watchman Nūr to rest?
And what about the time I rescued you
from death by crucifixion at the hands
of Būjahān the tyrant king of Ṣāḍḍ?

What other trials can you not recall
when you repelled the most vexatious threats
a saintly acolyte could ever face?'

The recollections soon began to flow
and flashes of emotional imprints
rekindled memories lost within the deep,
dark oceanic storehouse of my being.
'It cannot be… you're Ḥasākīn! But how?
A child of mother Gāiā, are you not?'

'The very same. I've taken many forms.
I am the one, the many. Long have I
accompanied your spirit as it roamed
the Maker's subtle and corporeal planes.

In every age, the clans of smokeless fire
have guided those who've praised the Merciful
and walked the hostile paths of axial saints.
And though the jinn and humankind remain
susceptible to wickedness and greed,
no two created races share as strong
a bond, or bear the burden of free will
the way we do.
           As beings of fire who roam
the planes and skies and oceans deep, we move
without the need to justify our own
existences, but move by Her decree
alone, compelled by Her engendering
and preternatural command of *'Be!'*
Absolved of blame, yet also free to roam.
Our wills are inextricably entwined.

Our own salvation is dependent on
the goodness and corruption that we sow
on Earth *and* in the isthmian domains,
for when the Real through whom creation blooms

shall gather us when measured Time expires,
and when the manifest totalities
are brought before the archangelic host
and placed upon the calibrated scales,
their lot shall either be accepted or
condemned to nonexistence, there to dwell
without reprieve.

We are custodians
of our Creator's singular opus.
To be the fixed North star that guides the flock
back to the fold of Her unrivalled grace
is our commitment to Her grand design.'

Resplendent Ḥasākīn then turned to me
and placed a fiery hand upon my cheek.
The coolness of the fire that licked my skin
surprised me. It was unlike anything
I'd ever felt before in either world.

'My dearest Āyā, you have never been
alone a single moment of your life.
You are my keep and my unbridled joy.
You are the zephyr whose sole origin
is Gāiā's Earth. You clear away the dust
of life that everyday accumulates
and bring relief to those in dire straits
and are a constant mercy to the worlds.
You are immutable. Remember that.'

'O Ḥasākīn!' I fell upon my knees
and wept prostrate. I pressed his fiery hand
upon my cheek and kissed it several times.

'How long, how long since we last parted ways!
I thought perhaps you had forgotten me
or left me stranded on the Zāgran planes

to roam untethered from my spirit guide.
But now, dear friend, I see you as you are
and gladness fills my being knowing that
you are substantially ubiquitous.

Though now I fear that our reunion may
presage another ominous portent
much like the mortal trials that I endured
throughout my wayfaring exploits on Earth.
But what's the meaning of my presence here?
What are the ciphers of this sacred house?
What cataclysmic code am I to crack?'

'I promise you, dear Āyā, all will be
duly revealed at the appointed time.
The Real through whom creation ever blooms
is also the All-Wise, All-Knowing One.
Be not despondent, but instead place all
your trust in Her and ply your fated course
and be receptive to theophanies.

The Bounteous Reality's cosmos
contains the multitudes, but so do you!
Remember that. Did She not say in Her
sublime Cylopiad that, out of all
the vessels in Creation, none contains
Her save the teeming hearts of devotees?
In far off lands, the sound philosophies
of gnostics have always identified
the heart as our storehouse of panoplies.

So, listen and receive those whisperings.
Do not discard a single murmur, no!
Each one relays a million myriads
of revelation pure, and knowledge of
the Names of that one named Reality.

Release the knot that tangles you and tie
your camel firmly to Her caravan,
and wheresoever your All-Knowing Guide
leads you, then that is where you're meant to be.'

≈≈≈≈≈≈≈≈

'I often wonder what it's like to be
a being of subtle nature like yourself.
Do jinn suffer the bitterness of death
as spirits with supreme ontologies?
Foul death that shall consume us one and all
when She unveils Her ultimate design,
when mighty Ursafīl, that great malāk,
shall sound her ancient horn and rip the veils,
when you and I and the entire train
of subtle and substantial beings of flesh
and smokeless fire are gathered rank and file
before the Real's supernal magistrates,
when both our kind will stand inert as each
and every word and deed is read aloud,
and none shall intercede on our behalf?

Will you not stand with me on equal grounds
to justify your own existence *then*?

And if your kind knows not the taste of death,
then why are you allowed to choose between
the oleander's poison or the boon
of Gāiā's everlasting banyan tree?'

'Would that you knew the truth behind it all,
that you shall never know the taste of death!
An earthly life is but a transient state.
Behold yourself. Observe how you exist
æthereally within this subtle sphere,
abstracted from the realm corporeal;

how you, through Her unerring Will remain
corporeous, and subtle as a wisp
of smoke that moves across the firmament.

I place my fiery hand upon your face
and hold you now, yet you remain unburned.
Is there a thing within the world of orbs,
or astral spheres that can resist pure fire—
which utterly consumes without remorse
the substance of all matter ever made?
Yet here you are uninjured and unmoved
as solid as the stone you're standing on.

Your consciousness enjoys the right to roam
the spheres of the imaginal sublime
the way mine does.

       We are exceedingly
endowed with privileges that beings of light
do not enjoy, for the malāʾika
are spheres within themselves. Their rarefied
materia prima self-satisfies
beyond all measure, as their substance flows
from out the well of immortality
that is the essence of the demiurges.

While they obey and issue from Her fount,
our own obey the Real's engendering
Command as firm subordinates of Her—
mere secondary causes journeying
in astral palanquins back to the first
primordial cause of cosmic enterprise.

And of our kind's susceptibility
to both the oleander's toxic fruit
as well as what is sweet and nourishing
like fig and quince and pomegranate seed

and all things good from Gāiā's realm to ours—
it all, in truth, means little in the end.

We are from Her—to Her we shall return.
The oleander fruit in paradise
is pure delight the way the banyan's fig
brings satisfaction to the partisans
condemned by merit to the House of Fire.

In Her sublime Cylopiad, the Real
is adamant and unequivocal
on matters of salvational decree:
that mercy is ensured, without a doubt,
extending not to some, but all of Her
beloved creations indiscriminately.
The vilest men to ever walk the Earth
cannot escape Her merciful embrace,
although they tried their best to sow discord,
to poison wells and fallow all Her fields.

Their true salvation is a thing assured,
to the dismay and misery of men
who claim to hold compassion in their hearts,
yet are, in truth, plain hypocrites who loathe
above all things unbounded Mercy's grace,
who do not see how dim their vision is
of virtue, ethics, and morality.'

≈≈≈≈≈≈≈≈

When finally we reached the end of that
enchantingly gratuitous expanse,
the doors then opened of their own accord.

We stepped into a most magnificent
high hall, upraised by wondrously ornate
Phystygian fluted columns shooting up

so high above our heads, had Ḥasākīn
not held me, I'd have fallen on my back.
I craned my head, and in astonishment
beheld the most exquisite canopy
I'd ever seen in any sphere.
                           It vied
with Her æthereal array of stars
for cosmic beauty and sheer majesty.

The canopy was masterfully inlaid
with some odd million shards of tesseræ.
Their sharp-cut edges glowed a shifting shade
of purply-blue that added to the dark
mystique of this entire temple.

                           Etched
upon the floor in calligraphic script
were Formulæ that glowed beneath my feet;
in fact, each single object that I touched
reacted with a glow that never failed
to startle me.
                     Serenely floating all
throughout the hall were jinn in flowing frocks
with lamps that burned with blue eternal flame.

Along the walls, and interspersed among
the columns, stood the bright ablution pools
of liquid light the monks would use to cleanse
themselves, conforming to the Real's prescript
of utmost piety, to execute
liturgical demands and sacred rites.

I watched a silent anchorite ahead,
not far away, with woven hood pulled back,
revealing flames like flowing locks that swirled
so handsomely against the dark.

>   I watched
him gather liquid light and douse his face
then diligently rinse both arms up to
his shoulders. As we passed him by, I heard
the anchorite reciting some scripture
beneath his breath, completely focused on
perfecting the ablution ritual.

'What ancient text is he reciting from?
Does humankind have any analogue?'

With infinite restraint, my guide replied:
'The mendicants of Gāiā's realm, who spend
their days meandering the planes alone
for years on end would surely recognize
that cryptic speech; for they alone among
mankind are fully versed in that unique
Monadic, archetypal dialect
first heard when pre-eternal Aleph loosed
the Letters from their mansions in the Great
Becoming, as narrated in the Real's
supernal and sublime Cylopiad.

Āyā, when you become the axial saint
of your epoch, the Absolute will grant
you passage to that same divine domain
that you may follow in the steps of your
esteemed prophetic line. The messengers
who walked the path and spread the news of Her
embody every archetype enshrined
in Her Cylopiad. They lived and breathed
and spoke and moved and ate and drank their fill
from Her deep springs of primal plenitude
while they dispelled corruption from the Earth
despite the mortal cost heaped onto them
oft by their own communities and kin.

Your time will come, and I'll be there with you,
when you shall stand before Mājūj the Fiend
and face the wrath of ages undeterred.

The tongue of the Unseen will be the blade
by which you end Mājūj's tyranny.'

≈≈≈≈≈≈≈≈

As Ḥasākīn continued to produce
successive pearls of rarefied insight,
we crossed the vast terrain of that great hall
then wandered through a mazy labyrinth
of endless vaults and silent colonnades.

We passed by modest chapels sheltering
small bands of jinnī anchorites who seemed
to be perpetually prostrate in prayer.
Their soft, incantatory Formulæ
reverberated all throughout the hall.
I breathed them in, and by some alchemy
I felt Firdaws' cleansing waters flow
through me, removing all residual
impurities I carried with me from
the world below.

　　　　The Names' obscure effects
induced a kind of subtle ecstasy
that overwhelmed my psychic faculties.
I squeezed my jinn companion's hand and asked
to pause for just a moment.

　　　　Ḥasākīn
then ushered me into a chapel, where
we sat beside some jinn in solemn prayer
and lingered for a while as I regained
my senses, and my soul returned from flight.

When I came to, I was enveloped by
the saintly anchorites' profound auras,
wherein I longed to bathe perpetually
in utter bliss for all eternity.

≈≈≈≈≈≈≈≈

I wondered whether this enchanting sphere
was governed by the laws of Time or not,
and whether jinn necessitated rest,
for even fire requires some kind of fuel!
While fuel emits a residue as proof
that it's consumed, these pre-eternal jinn—
they leave no char as evidence at all
but swirling flames of rare and radiant gold.
The jinn are truly a perplexing race!

Perhaps the thing that I admired most
about the noble jinn was how obsessed
they were with mastering a sacred rite;
and how the ritual of any task
they tackled purified them to a high
degree entirely unknown to us
low beings.

        Our own substance corrupts
from birth, for watery clay's our origin.
Excess of any kind disintegrates
our composition necessarily.

For all I knew, whole eons came and went
before we left the chapel and resumed
our quest to reach the queen of all the clans.

Although I was a bit disoriented
by our repose—however long it was—
a totally renewed resolve combined

with pure child-like excitement to explore
compelled my spirit and impelled my feet
to glide as swiftly as the jinnī float.

We made our way through several halls replete
with basins full of light that shone like pearls
whose pools reflected off the stony walls.

Adorning all the entryways were shields
that bore the names of all the different clans
in splendidly ornate calligraphy:
the house of Rāqi of the seventh sphere,
the houses of Bulkān and Ṣafaḍī
and Ṭūs and Būjā of the fourteenth sphere
and Ṭūmar of the sphere of eminence
and that most honored house of Jarjawayn,
whose sphere of no-sphere reigns above the rest.

Each hall displayed the statues of its chiefs—
great sackers of empires who reigned supreme
and led victorious campaigns against
barbaric hordes who sowed discord on the Earth.

Between the statues, there were niches in
the walls with ornate terracotta jars
detailed with vibrant shades of indigo
turquoise, azure, and jade, with wondrous scenes
of famous battles, each embellished with
choice lines from epic poems by Ṣādūr
who's Heliopic hanging odes brought fame
eternal to the line of Rā'issā.

We crossed the great pylon of Dār Ḥakīm
and entered an ablution vestibule
with a majestic fount of liquid light
and softly chanting jinn with rolled up sleeves
performing their prescribed ablution rites

required of them upon entry. I felt
compelled to cleanse myself, and so I did,
from head to toe, along with Ḥasākīn
who led me in reciting all the Names
correctly, and by rank and magnitude.

The liquid light felt even cooler than
the frigid fire of jinn. My hands went numb,
but then the numbness went away and left
me feeling a degree of purity
I'd never felt before.
     I doused myself
indecorously at first, then reverently.
I focused on reciting every Name
that Ḥasākīn uttered impeccably
and on fulfilling the ablution rites
down to the finest, most minute detail.

An urge arrested me, and so I asked
my guide if I could drink the liquid light.
He nodded with a smile, and so I took
 a sip
   and instantly experienced
an overwhelming theophanic flash
so numbingly intense that I refrained
from drinking more than what was good for me.

He knew that I was in over my head
the moment I shot him a yearning glance.

Though soothing to the souls of axial saints,
the heat of near annihilation burns
the throats of ignorant novitiates
pursuing what is not permitted them.

≈≈≈≈≈≈≈≈

Once cleansed, we exited the vestibule
onto a sprawling upper terrace flanked
by brooding sphinxes posing regally
and nāwrī trees of sacred origin
with luminescent, pendulous branchlets
that swayed prostrate with great humility.

Above us was a dark empyrean
that teemed with stars and moons and galaxies
and gaseous clouds of opalescent light
that formed a dazzling cosmic tapestry
I recognized immediately from past
experiences while roaming isthmian
landscapes of the imaginal third eye —
all but confirming my suspicion that,
in this abode, we were unmoored from Time,
and were ever engulfed in cryptic night.

From that high terrace, we were able to
look on the whole complex — a glorious sight!
I marveled at the striking masonry
in full display and thought
                              how cruel it was
that this immense astral display lay so
beyond the cloudy veil of human sight.

Each rare convexity, concavity,
contour and curvature my eyes took in
adhered to one eternal ratio
perceptible in all engendered forms
in every ontological domain —
of this, my guide made sure I was aware.

Along the limestone path I walked upon
were hieroglyphs enlaced with brilliant lines
from Ḥawthī's greatest epic, *Balgarām* —
the finest poem in the Kūfic tongue —

a poem so profoundly beautiful
the demiurges themselves would lose their minds,
stone-drunk on these mythic hagiographies
of battle-worn epic heroes and gods
in scintillating rhymed heptameter.

A warm blue light from floating oil lamps
illuminated our precipitous
descent down to the lower terraces,
where ample pleasure gardens greeted us
with nāwrī, fig and honeysuckle trees,
majestic founts of flowing liquid light,
and royal guard of jinn praetorians
in full regalia flanked along the path
that led directly to the citadel's
main entryway into the anteroom
of Queen Ashtūrumāzda's royal court.

We entered through omniscient, heaving doors
that opened automatically as soon
as we arrived.

       Inside the anteroom
were vast frescos of ancient matriarchs
of Queen Ashtūrumāzda's noble house.
Their faces shimmered in the blue lamplight
emitting from the niches in the walls.

The final scenes from Ḥawthī's *Balgarām*—
they culminated at the court's entrance
upon the massive, ornate double doors.
The calligraphic verses wrapped around
an illustration of Bint ʿĀshurāʾ
the warrior queen, her foot pressed down upon
the heads of vanquished foes of flesh and fire.

Those mighty doors then opened on their own
and there she was, the queen of all the clans
sat poised on her resplendent, lofty throne
with adamantine scepter planted firm,
surrounded by her many jinn courtiers—
commanders of her armies, grand wazīrs,
imperial bodyguards and chancellors,
her ministers of war and public works,
administrators of her treasuries,
her scribes, her central secretariat,
her grand preceptors, poet laureates,
high priests, their many mystic acolytes,
philosophers and theologians
from sovereign territories far and wide,
cup-bearing houri boys of jinn aspect
and slaves with heads bowed low in deference to
their queen and her imperial retinue.

I followed close behind my jinnī guide
and crossed the sacred threshold reverently
with eyes averted and my head bowed down.
The queen knocked twice with her scepter, and all
arose to greet us as we slowly inched
toward the dais.

       I was so afraid
and so intimidated by the whole
occasion that I hid behind my guide,
but Ḥasākīn, who sensed my nervousness,
turned 'round, gave me a reassuring smile,
then took my hand and pulled me by his side.

We both humbly prostrated there before
our splendid host, who struck the ground again
with her scepter, and all the courtiers sat
as Ḥasākīn then helped me to my feet.

'My queen, great hostess of our citadel,
O sovereign of sovereigns, O lord of lords,
supreme ruler of all the subtle spheres
and all who dwell within their astral planes!
I bring glad tidings from the lower realm—
a true ally and pearl among mankind
and future axial saint of her epoch,
the incorruptible disciple of
Yāsīn, the son of Roā—Messenger
of the...'

The queen then raised her hand to cut him off,
then beckoned me to introduce myself.

I stood there for a moment, petrified.
The pin-drop silence felt like crushing walls
collapsing over me.

                    'I am Āyā
the Heliopolite, and I am yours
entirely, O queen of all the clans,
most favored sovereign of the Merciful.
Direct your humble slave as you see fit
that I may enter paradise fulfilled.'

'The zephyrs carry news of you, Āyā,
that infiltrates the isthmian membranes
that separate the worlds of flesh from fire.'

Her thunderous voice echoed throughout the court,
dramatically increasing my distress.
I dared not lift my head to look at her,
such was my fear of seeming even half
of an iota too indecorous.

'Look on me, child, 'tis no affront at all,
but be at ease and speak freely with me,
and honestly,

for the All-Knowing knows
and measures every kernel you conceal
within the confines of your mystic heart,
and She is clement and all-merciful
and just rewards await the virtuous.

So, tell me, Āyā, what have you discerned
through journeying behind the subtle veils
regarding essences and sound gnosis,
and does it correlate with what the sage
philosophers have offered us in kind?'

I felt the searing heat of every glare
acutely, rising in severity
with every passing moment standing there.

I closed my eyes, attempted to regain
composure, then I called upon the Real
to ease my burden and to guide my tongue
and satisfy my host with measured words:

'When veils and their essential qualities
forfeit their treasuries, and zephyrs drive
the pure well-springs primordial to rend
the dam of She/not she, beings shall flee
their bodies ere they lose their necks in flight
from peak to peak, from pole to axial pole,
unmoored from idle talk of journeying.'

There was a pregnant pause so vacuous,
it swiftly sucked the air from out the court.
A few courtiers in shock drew startled breaths
that led me to believe my time was nigh,
that my excessively complacent, frank
response offended my imperious host.

The queen then broke the silence as she rose
from her high throne, and every courtier rose

immediately in kind.
                   She floated down
with grace, then sat upon the lowest step
which drew more startled breaths from stunned courtiers
who'd never witnessed their empress debase
herself before a pitiful subject,

a partisan of clay, no less, with whom
she now sat eye-to-eye.

                     She placed both hands
on her scepter, leaned forward and betrayed
a slight, disarming smile, relieving me
of my insufferable anxieties.

'It seems like you've been knocking on the door
of gnosis with persistence and intent
beyond the years you've briefly been alive.
The Generous has justifiably
rewarded you.
                  It is unusual
for beings of flesh to even have access
to these obscure celestial domains.
Yāsīn and Ḥasākīn have guided you
impeccably thus far. I am impressed.'

'I'm truly humbled by your words, my queen.
My own wayfaring journey is to serve
the Real through whom creation ever blooms,
and beings of clay and light and smokeless fire
are creatures most sublime, for we receive
            supererogatory messages
through Her esteemed prophets and axial saints
and have the will to choose the paths we trod.'

The queen's eyes widened, and her interest piqued.
She snapped her fingers, and three servants brought

a plush dīvān for us to rest upon.

'And of our kind? What has the Merciful
revealed to you about the folk of fire?'

I knew it wasn't, but I couldn't help
the feeling that this was some sort of trap.
Tread softly, Āyā, lest it be your life!

'Before the Grand Event, in that epoch
of pre-eternity, before the Cry
of Aleph loosed the Letters from their state
of dormancy within the sacred womb
of their exalted mansions,
                              in the sphere
of no sphere, the Engenderer conceived
and fashioned from a subtle, hylic flame
the primogenitor of all the jinn.

And when the hour struck, the demiurge
then summoned three sublime malāʾika
who formed from nothing six impeccable
æthereal spheres exclusive to the jinn.

The Real then charged those same malāʾika
to regulate the fashioning of all
the jinn, according to Her sound designs.
The age of smokeless fire was imminent.

The three malāʾika approached the one
existing jinn configured by the Real,
and cleaved its body open, wedding one
part to the other,
                       and the two produced
offspring, and their offspring had offspring too.

They soon split into twelve initial tribes
that further fractured into smaller clans.

As eons passed, the clans grew envious
and wars were waged between them, brutal wars
of genocidal carnage.
                    Several clans
were wiped away, and those that did survive
were decimated, and the barbarous age
of cyclical blood feuds reigned over them.'

I briefly paused,
                  then lost my train of thought.

'My queen, I have no need to lecture you
on lineages or histories of wars
between kinfolk, for I have seen them etched
in frescos all throughout this citadel.

We're blessed to have you reign victorious
against the hordes of jānn—the horrid crew,
the mix-flamed foes resigned to causing ill
throughout the subtle cosmic hierarchies.

Their apoplectic hatred of your kind
was born of jealous rage against the Real
who fashioned jinn in pre-eternity
of smokeless fire most rarified and pure,
while they themselves are admixtures of flame
whose residue is witnessed in whirlwinds
throughout the lower realms of humankind—
such is the state of their impurity.
They are forsaken by the Absolute
and non-existence is their fated lot—
their House of Fire for all eternity.

Beneath your yoke, empress, they are resigned
to wallowing between the realms of clay
and nothingness, condemned to serpentine
scheming for all-out war against the worlds.'

The wide-eyed queen looked ponderously at me,
while drum-tapping the top of her scepter.
She snapped her fingers once again.
        The sound
echoed throughout the hall, and houri jinn
in haste brought jewel-encrusted chalices
of liquid light for Ḥasākīn and I.

I stared into my cup and gently swirled
the radiant liquid light. Her highness sensed
my apprehensiveness immediately.

'Don't be afraid, for like the loathsome jānn,
it is a mixed dilution easily
dispensed with. Drink wayfarer. To your health!'

I waited for the queen to sip her drink
before I raised my chalice to my lips.
To my relief, the cool elixir washed
away the nerves, and pure felicity
reigned over my sensorial faculties.

'The Heliopolites refer to you
by many names—Āyā the whisperer,
avenging Āyā, lion tamer, lamb
of the arena and the like. I want
to hear the tale directly from the source
precisely how you earned such epithets.'

I wished to drain my cup at once to numb
the pain of sharing my traumatic tale
that, like a demon, haunts me night and day.

I looked at Ḥasākīn, who read my mind,
aware of my distress. 'Go on,' he said
in silent code, 'just one more beast to tame.'

'These epithets are accurate, my queen.
They follow me like mud beneath my feet.
I seem to track them everywhere I go.

They live as ill reminders of a life
that was no life, but slow decay—a sheer
erasure of my sovereign personhood.

I was betrothed by force to some praetor
of noble rank with regal pedigree
three times my age
                    of fifteen at the time—
a daughter of a tanner who had died
from inhalation merely weeks before
the fateful day my mother took me out
to greet the troops of our great Paterōn
on their return from their victorious
campaign against the rebels of Yusrāw.

The roaring mob,
                the swirl
        of burning myrrh
        and fragrant agar wood,
                            the acrobats,
the wailing,
                ululating
                        choruses,
the patriotic anthems bellowing,
the belting sun,
                    the sweat of bodies all
around me,
                mother pushing me between
them, desperate to be right along the path
as close to the parade as possible.

We ploughed through everyone.

                      I was the ram
misused to batter through the shifting mob
of bodies 'til we reached the very edge
of all the action and cacophony.

My mother cheered the stream of regiments
with stupefying verve and foaming zeal
that frightened me.

                  The whole affair oppressed
and smothered me. I wanted to go home,
I was in tears, I felt ensnared, assailed
and impotent, unable to resist,

but she was so enraptured by it all.
I felt I had no choice but to relent,
and so, I stood there apprehensively
and watched the ranks of festooned troops march
through the massive gates of Heliopolis.

When I look back, I want to curse the sands
of Time, I vex the moment and the sight
that shifted *the* most shifting eyes of men
toward this child amid the roaring throng—
a thing in waiting ready to be plucked.

And when he entered my immediate sphere
my nostrils burned, assaulted by the reek
of this feral, desert-marauding brute.
The praetor, with a salivating smile
more serpentine than anything, kneeled down
then introduced himself as Minas son
of Dāmarkand, then asked me for my name.
I turned away and clutched my mother's side.

'Her name's Āyā, my lord. You honor us!'
She bowed before the praetor, forcing me
to do the same.
                    I cursed him as I did.

In rapid time, the two of them dispensed
with pleasantries ere moving onto more
transactional affairs.
                    Intentions were
affirmed, the deal was struck, and like a lamb
condemned to slaughter, all prospects of life
were in that moment rendered null and void.

As I look back on those inflection points,
I recognize the sharp vicissitudes
cruel Fate felt fit to have us face alone
since my poor father's slow and tortured death,
and so, I understand her rationale.

Through me, she'd seize the opportunity
to elevate her status and remove
her from the widow's state of poverty—
a single mother with an only child
with deep financial insecurities
that loom and threaten to destroy her life.

Such monumental opportunities
as fleeting as a flicker, come but once,
then, in a flash, they fade away like smoke;
so prudent folk best be prepared to pounce
unhesitatingly, with murderous
intent if they're to seize the prize they crave—
a life of ease and rank cupidity.

I wanted none of it.

          The piety
my mother superficially displayed
in public spheres, in me was most sincere
for I had tasted from an early age
that wine of pre-eternal origin.

My father, bless him, was a pious man
in whom the light of Self-disclosure shone
so radiantly, it melted hearts like wax,
and he was so receptive to the Signs
and messages the Real relayed to him,
and he embodied them, and he was kind,
and humbler than a sandal-bearing saint.

Besides my mother, father's dearest mate
was Seyyid Bin Sufyān, the blind ʿaṭṭār
and sage of our Old Quarter alleyway.

The tanner and ʿaṭṭār spent every day
together in the market, selling hides
and spices from adjoining dakākīn.

And in the night, the Seyyid's residence
would function as a mystic meeting house
where he'd receive a stream of aspirants
the whole year through, who'd come from near and far
to sit at Seyyid's feet and hear firsthand
accounts from five decades of journeying
across the sprawling planes of Gāiā's Earth,

such as the tale of his encounter with
the famous Khiżr, when Seyyid Bin Sufyān
had found precisely where the two seas meet
but never mingle,

              or accounts of his
exchanges with anointed messengers

and prophets as they drank from Kawthar's pure,
supernal spring,
                    or of his travels through
the spheres when, like Burāq, he would ascend
and in a single night return from flight.

≈≈≈≈≈≈≈≈

When I was old enough to apprehend
the subtle signs of Her Cylopiad
and demonstrate my knowledge of the Truth,
my father started taking me along
to Seyyid Bin Sufyān's evening conclaves,
and when the last wayfarer left his home,
I'd sit with them—my father and Sufyān—
and listen avidly as they engaged
in lengthy theological debates,
or reminisced and pined for simpler times

before the current Paterōn's long reign
of tyranny began, when he declared
himself dictator in perpetuum
some thirty years ago or thereabouts.
It was a dire event,
                    or so they claimed.
For me, it was but antique history.

My father and the Seyyid often took
me with them to go circumambulate
the Banyan Tree and sit among the folk
of subtle thought who gathered 'round Sufyān
as he took rest by the communal fount
beneath the portico of Rex Ḥanbal.

It was on one of these occasions that
I heard my very first cipher or sign
directly from the isthmian domain

of perfect Forms and hanging Images.

It was a Self-disclosure by the Real
through whom creation blooms, a subtle trace
made manifest by the All-Merciful,
delivered by an emissary of
the lonely reed that longed to be restored
to its primordial source of Vast Earth mud.

It was the moment I became aware
of King Huthayfa and the Ḥarakite:
Yāsīn, the son of Roā—Messenger
and Prophet of the Most Compassionate.

It was the moment everything had changed
for me.

        I knew, as if I'd always known,
that mine was only half a soul, that I
was substance lacking every quality,
and he was all the qualities in one
perfected form, both comely and sublime.

I took my father by the hand and sped
toward the two, 'round whom a modest crowd
had gathered—mostly adolescent youths—
and sat among them.

        Even Bin Sufyān—
who recognized the subtlest of signs
and heard the ciphered music of the spheres
with ears the Merciful fine-tuned Herself—
sat down and listened carefully to what
Yāsīn was sharing with the former king
regarding matters of the guiding lights,
and of the uncreated codices
in which the Real encoded Her divine
Cylopiad for all eternity.

He spoke about the cosmic enterprise
of Names and how they manifest to us
in traces, and their teleological
relationships with the observable
cosmos,

       and of the Gatherer, who raised
the vaults of Gāiā's Earth, and who arranged
the lunar and sublunar realms by rank,
and fixed the stations and celestial realms
by magnitude and by proximity
to the Possessor of the Final Hour.

His exegesis of the final verse —
my *favorite* verse — of the Cylopiad
provoked an epiphanic episode
so utterly intense, it left me out
of body, out of mind, entirely
annihilated in the wine-dark sea
of Her primordial Reality.

When I came to, the stars had realigned.
The hylic matter of the universe
transformed from mud to manna from on high,
and my complete terrestrial landscape
had turned into an oceanic realm
of perfect Forms, ciphers and sacred Names.

       I've sailed no other firmament
          since then.

≈≈≈≈≈≈≈≈

When we returned that night, I couldn't sleep.
I was annihilated by the pure
and potent drink reserved exclusively
for those who shun the world in favor of

a life devoted to embodying
the Names,

       and having tasted it, I thence
became among the folk who yearn for wine
from Gāiā's native land exclusively,

for what on Earth is there that can replace
the taste of that celestial vintage—
wine-pressed from the apocalyptic fruit?

       ≈≈≈≈≈≈≈≈

When father died not long thereafter, life
itself had lost all purpose, and as I
was overcome by sorrow and despair,
I'd steal away at night in desperate need
of healing, and the only remedy
was being in the sanctum with Yāsīn
and listening to him unveil with grace
and clarity the Master's archetypes,
and, so, the Sanctuary offered me
a space to grieve and gradually revive.

My life came under greater scrutiny
when I was sold to Minas as a bride,
and sneaking out at night proved challenging,

but nothing could have kept me from Yāsīn.
I always found a way.

       By accident
one night, my mother caught me sneaking back
into the house
       and laid a violent blow
on me that broke my jaw
       in what was quite
a gruesome scene.

Straight to my room I fled,
leaving a bloody trail behind.

I fumed
the whole night through as that horrific scene
replayed over and over in my mind.

Soon thoughts would shift from penetrating pain
and misery to unconditional
rebellion.

Numb with rage, I strategized
and plotted well into the early hours
until a foolproof plan was fully formed.

As soon as I saw light from Qurashī
the baker's window, it was time to go.

I made my way through quiet alleyways,
clandestine as a shadowy Ḥashāsh—
a whisp of smoke unerring in its course.

I soon was sat in blessedness beneath
the Banyan in the presence of Yāsīn,
Huthayfa and my fellow devotees.

≈≈≈≈≈≈≈

The frequency of those returning to
Yāsīn with diverse injuries sustained
in incidents identical to mine
alarmed him, for he knew he was the cause
that led to these disturbing incidents.

He sought to mitigate the damage done,
though it required divulging hidden things
from hidden realms reserved for higher beings.

Just days before, in utter disbelief,
I watched Yāsīn repair a broken arm
before my eyes there by the Banyan Tree.
I swear on Gāiā's grave, within the course
of those few days, I watched him heal the kinds
of injuries that even our most skilled
physicians would have deemed inoperable.

When I approached him with my broken jaw
on that most dire day of consequence,
    I too became a beneficiary.

        ≈≈≈≈≈≈≈≈

Yāsīn's overt, bewildering displays
within the sanctum of the holy shrine
were ill-received.

          The rumors quickly spread
of some possessed apostate foreigner
performing sacrilegious sorcery
within the sanctum of the Master's House,
whose sole intent was to corrupt the minds
of unsuspecting Heliopolites.

When members of more prominent estates
assembling 'round Huthayfa and Yāsīn
increased, so did the violent rhetoric
that called for every Heliopolite
to do what's right and drive away the pair
of wretched foreigners affronting them;
to cleanse the sacred shrine by any means—
the laws be damned! for this was truly dire.

        ≈≈≈≈≈≈≈≈

The hostile atmosphere engulfing us,
though palpable, did nothing to dissuade
us from enjoying our most sacred right
as Zāgran citizens:
                     to seek refuge
beneath the shade of Gāiā's Banyan Tree—
the symbol of religious tolerance—
within the safety of our sacred shrine.

The peace was shattered and the space profaned
when Minas and my mother stormed into
the sanctuary, outing me among
the group.
                The praetor seized me by the arm
to forcibly remove me, but I seized
him back.
                I grabbed his tunic, and I tore
it from the collar down, exposing his
unseemly nakedness,
                     and Minas was
humiliated thoroughly before
a massive crowd of gawking witnesses.

I can't remember anything beyond
that point.
                The vengeful praetor struck me down
and I lost consciousness.
                  From what I'm told
he beat me viciously with such unhinged
and blinding rage, he couldn't stem his cruel
assault until he practically collapsed
from sheer exhaustion.
                  Mother, like a stone,
stood there and watched, expressionless and cold.

The praetor took a moment to regain
composure,
                wiped my blood from off his hands
and face, then grabbed me by my hair and dragged
my broken body from the sanctum through
the streets and alleys,
                        all the way to Dār
Mutaqqal prison three districts away
where I awoke after a day or two
in iron chains
                abused beyond belief.

With broken arms and legs and shattered jaw,
I needed to be dragged before the Dār
Mutaqqal martial court and sat before
a magistrate of hoary men who laid
against me several counts of truly wild
concocted charges.

                None of them meant much
to me—a mangled child of fifteen years:

Assault against a royal officer,
conspiring to commit assault against
a royal officer, offense against
the state, defacing public property
of cultural and sacred heritage—
the last few counts relating to blood spilled
in the assault that splattered all around
the sanctum—
                a profane blood sacrifice
beneath the altar of the Banyan Tree.

The only thing that pierced through all the noise
was 'Death by public execution.' I
was set to be the sacrificial lamb—
the main event to culminate a week

of celebrating, fittingly, the day
of sacrificial slaughter, honoring
the prophet Ruzbihān of Azra Kāf.

They dragged me back to jail, placed iron chains
back on my feet and left me there to rot
for two more days 'til I was due to die.
It was a shame. I'd turn sixteen in three.

Yāsīn and my newfound companions, led
by Ṣamaḍī, who bribed the prison guards,
slipped into my appalling prison cell,
and from then on, they didn't leave my side
until the moment came that forced them to
evade the guards tasked with transporting me
to the Colossei Gladitorium.

In those two days, Yāsīn did what he could
to mend my bones and fix my jaw again,
employing his alchemic faculties
at full capacity—a grueling task—
with time to work depleting rapidly.

They nurtured me, each one of them, 'til I
could sit upright and talk to them without
the biting pain that coupled every move.

Alas, it was a short-lived luxury
to be with them until the very last
before my life's thin thread was to be cut
so prematurely and theatrically.

As they departed from my cell, Yāsīn
came close and whispered words into my ear
to give as pittance to the ferryman
before my final crossing back to Her
primordial realm of pure beatitude.

His words expelled the last remaining dregs
of fear I had of death within my heart.
I was at last prepared for martyrdom.

≈≈≈≈≈≈≈

At noon, imperial guards came in, restrained
me, forcing me upright. They dragged me out
of Dār Mutaqqal and paraded me
through Heliopolis.

                My dismal train
was an overt procession of extreme
humiliation, lasting all the way
to the Colossei Gladitorium,
where I assumed I would be stoned or mauled
or crucified according to the law.

Inside the vomitorium they threw
me up against a wall, spread out my arms
and legs, placed iron shackles on my wrists
attached to chains that dangled down from hooks,
then tore my tunic from the collar down,
exposing me.

                They brought a bleating lamb
before me, inhumanely slaughtered it
in dedication to the deity,
then painted me in sacrificial blood
from head to toe.

                The stench of excrement,
wet hay and gore was positively vile.
It stung my passages and filled my lungs
and worse! the taste that lingered on my tongue.

The thunderous roar of Heliopolites
that flooded through the bolted traps assailed

my ears but struck no fear in me at all.
I was impervious, immovable.
I scoffed at fear! for I had words to give
to that agèd Tartarian ferryman
who soon would ferry me across the Maout.

The traps crashed open. Sunlight hit my eyes
and briefly blinded me. I was unhooked
and by my blood-soaked hair, they dragged me out
into the great arena.
                              I was met
by the unreal, uproarious thunderclap
of some three hundred thousand strong in force,
full-throated, baying, foaming at the mouth,
demanding to be entertained or else.

They tied me to a mighty stake that stood
at center-stage, its splintery surface slit
my skin—I felt the blood drip down my wrists.

The blare of coronets cut through the din,
announcing the arrivals of elect
imperial courtiers filing out by rank
along the sheltered terraces on high,

the last of whom was praetor Minas, son
of Dāmarkand, my mother close behind.

Five hidden traps crashed open all at once
and from their subterranean cells leapt out
four massive lions and a lioness.
Three hundred thousand Heliopolites
erupted all at once. I'd never heard
so deafening a sound before nor since.

They paced around me, goaded by the mob
who threw projectiles at them, pelting them
with stones, with sandals, wineskins, and the like

to agitate and urge them to attack.
They started closing in with odious
intent, producing deep and guttural growls.

A male approached. He snarled and bared his teeth
and I bared mine. He roared at me and I
roared back, as if possessed by some shayṭān.
I'd grown impatient. I was in a rush
to pay my pittance to the ferryman
and cross the Maout as soon as possible.

The manic crowd began their chants of 'kill!'
The lion was within a few bows' length.
It pawed the dirt and gave a heaving huff,
then pounced on me in one explosive move!
but he was intercepted, caught beneath
the neck by the audacious lioness.

The two enormous beasts came tumbling down
to Earth in a tremendous haze of dust.
She left her gruesome mark and he fell back.

The women in the crowd threw their support
behind the lioness and me. At once
the focus shifted from unanimous
desire to see a child be torn apart
to savage war of sexes to the death.

The lions flanked the lioness and pounced.
Their tangled bodies tumbled down to Earth—
a cloud of carnal chaos most profound.
As fang and claw sunk into flesh and blood,
the heinous cries of slaughter shattered through
the utterly obscene, ear-splitting din
of the Colossei Gladitorium.
They tore into the lioness and turned
her into carrion—a gory heap

devoid of pity, strewn across the plane.
Her entrails glistened in the noon-day sun.

The glutted crowd then grew fanatical,
continuing their raucous chants of "kill!"
They goaded on the males, who tore away
from lioness and set their sights on me.

As they approached, I felt no hint of fear.
I was fed up with this protracted game.
I shut my eyes as tightly as I could,
implored the Expediter to mete out
Her sentence and dispense with me at once.

The chants of "kill!" were suddenly replaced
by whistles, jeers and curses, coupled with
projectiles raining down from every tier.
When I opened my eyes, the lions lay
before me, paws outstretched and heads bowed down.

The injured one benignantly approached.
He circled 'round me once then brushed his mane
against my legs, fell at my feet and rolled
onto his side like some supine housecat.

The traps crashed open once again. This time
the lion handlers were tossed out of them
and left defenseless as the traps slammed shut
behind them.
             All four lions turned toward
their handlers and immediately attacked.
They pitilessly tore them limb from limb.

The glutted crowd vociferously roared
in satisfaction. Moments later, ten
well-armored pikemen burst onto the scene.
They flooded out in fixed formation, hemmed
the lions in, then skewered them one by one

between the eyes. Brain matter, blood and gore
spewed out their skulls as spears were wrenched away
with vicious, maximal brutality.

By then I'd earned the crowd's support in full,
both men and women. Thousands of them scaled
the ineffective barriers and spilled
into the carnage-mangled killing field
with murder in their eyes.
                              They fast engulfed
the pikemen and impaled them with their spears.
The mob then shifted their hostilities
toward the gentry in the galleries
and lobbed still more projectiles and insults.

I spotted Minas on the highest tier
with mother by his side, surrounded by
the stately plutocrats she idolized.
The praetor's eyes met mine. I felt the heat
of his vexatious gaze filled with contempt.
He seized my mother from behind and slit
her throat from ear to ear.
                              He then looked down
at me, then kept on cutting 'til her head
was severed from her body.
                              Minas thrust
the blade into her breast then threw her head
down to the pit below and disappeared.

Amid the chaos, someone put their arms
around me. It was Ḥakkān Ṣamaḍī,
Huthayfa and Yāsīn. I threw my arms
around them and we left the stadium
escorted by the son of Ṣamaḍī,
who parted the entire crowd with ease
as they fell back before his eminence.'

≈≈≈≈≈≈≈≈

Throughout the court, a silence most profound.
My tale had robbed the air from out the room.
I looked around and momentarily,
ecstatically lost sense of time and place.

The jinnī queen, as stoic as a stone,
hunched over, chin in hand, then sat upright.
She ushered me to come up close to her.
I did as she commanded cautiously,
averting all the while my heedful gaze.

She gently raised my head with her index,
insistent that I look into her eyes—
each one, a swirling, metacosmic pool
that sucked me in and left me hypnotized.

'The lions—how did you spell-bind the beasts?'
The frigid-fiery touch of her index,
like liquid light, sent shivers down my spine.
I took a moment to compose myself.

'I had nothing to do with it, my queen.
It was Yāsīn who asked Elia the arch-
angelic being to intercede on my
behalf by speaking to the lions in
the subtle isthmian vernacular.
His intercession spared me on the day.'

She placed her hand upon my cheek and smiled—
the frigid fire felt cool and comforting.

'The forces that surround you vindicate
your mission and your purpose in these worlds.
The lunar spheres are deeply envious
that Gāiā's Earth should be your native land.
Your narrative capacities outshine

the ancient bards of Ṭūs and Azra Kāf,
matched only by your knowledge of divine
realities that you've inherited
from every shepherd who has guided you.'

'You truly honor me, my queen, beyond
what I deserve. The only thing I have
in common with the righteous messengers,
prophets and saints, is having never asked
to carry out a mission well beyond
my means.

      We humans never stood a chance
without sublime or supernatural aid
to save us from our own destructive selves,
and those like me, again, who never asked
to bear the burden of humanity,
must persevere or suffer martyrdom.

We have no other choice but to survive,
and subtle interventions by the Real
through whom Creation blooms eternally
and Her vicegerents sent from every sphere
bring light into a twilit, fallen world
in desperate need of recognizing Her
in every aspect hid and manifest.

When we begin to hear Her dulcet song
in every subtle sound, or see Her face
in everything, wherever, all the time,
or lend our voices as a vehicle,
or heed Her prophecies sent down to us,

we may begin, both jinn and partisans
of clay, to fully justify our own
existences, that we may benefit,
reset the scales and walk the straightened path.

We are from Her—to Her we shall return,
for She is pre-and-post eternity,
the infinite—the Necessary Being.

The Great Becoming spawned the demiurges
who fractured into tribes the moment they
were born into the great chaotic cloud,
and from the start, the demiurges were prone
to losing their innate capacities
of recognizing any trace of Her,
all due to dissipating memories
of their divine primordial origins.

As they adventured through the cosmic cloud,
they designated eight primordials—
the Essence and the seven Attributes
of Her sublime sensorial faculties,

but they were ignorant, for nothing is
primordial but one, and She is One,
and She is the exalted Real, for She
is oneness absolute in all aspects
and there is no reality but Her.

I am illusion plain, human, corrupt,
but all the ancient entities of fire
received the first command to bow before
a thing of clay that from Her Breath gained life.

The thirty-thousand mysteries behind
that cataclysmic moment will remain
obscure 'til our Return to Her domain.

Yet there must be a reason we were deemed
redeemable, exalted from the start!

My queen, I've forfeited all agency
to our sublime Mover of astral forms,

to every guide, beginning with Yāsīn,
inheritor of Names and treasuries,
to Sākina, our epoch's axial saint,
to Ḥasākīn and Gāiā's living seed,
who've led me now to you, the queen of all
the clans of fire across the hierarchies.

The zephyrs blow throughout the subtle spheres,
and through the vast vistas of Gāiā's Earth.
They carry coded messages from Her,
reminding us that our supernal home
is found within the kernels of our hearts—
the only organ able to confine
the essences of Names and Attributes.

They are the multitudes that we contain
within our beings' deepest cavities,
which are identical to multitudes
made manifest within the cosmic cloud
within which we are totally contained—
the hidden and the manifest—that which
is both within us and without, just as
the sage Barāhima philosophized
in their prodigious scrolls of great import.

We all participate in a renewed
creation of the hierarchies entire,
at every instant, bursting from the fount
of Self-disclosure unrelentingly.

I'm but a secondary accident,
a rogue explorer in a cosmic sea.

When my emprises in the worlds conclude,
and I retire this fleshly form for good,
I hope to say that my distinct impress
on Gāiā's Earth and her communities

was helping people recognize Her face
and see Her Signs across the vaulted domes,
across the two horizons of the dark
empyrean, in the subtle fineries
of fauna, flora and whatever dwells
below the firmament and in the skies,
to look inwardly for the Master's key
to unlock every treasury there is.

The rest is pittance for the ferryman.
May he be satisfied and ferry well
when we arrive to cross the River Maout.'

The queen sat up and drew the gaze of all
the courtiers still in shock from seeing her
debase herself before a being of clay.
With minimal gestures, her eminence
dismissed the brooding courtiers one and all,
and Ḥasākīn, the queen and I were left
alone in that resplendent court, where we
shared drafts of liquid light and knowledge of
the essences and veils, of stations high
and low and all the riches they contain,
of Self-disclosure, Signs and their loci,
of nonexistent entities, waymarks,
and noble orders of infinity,
of knowledge of the absent witnesser,
and of the Breath of the All-Merciful
for several hours on end 'til it was time
for my return to Gāiā's resting place
to reunite with my corporeal form.

Before my guide prepared me for descent,
her majesty the queen conferred on me
an ancient relic—Cāto's calamus—
then offered me an honorary seat

of high esteem among her retinue,
made Ḥasākīn my guardian for life,
and ere we left, commissioned me to write
an epic fit to stand the test of Time
to elevate the art and honor her.

The Isthmus

Wayfarers ask me constantly concerning
    the in-between.
What then should I say to them?
    To know is *not* to know?

I am no keeper of gates, nor a boudoir-
    guarding eunuch
refusing unsuitables entry
    to a garden of many waters.

Out of desperation they refuse
    none other than themselves,
thinking they might slip through
    the veil actively
when passive receptivity
    is required to gain entry.

≈≈≈≈≈≈≈≈

A youth from Bounān
    in the Northern Yusrāw hinterlands
asked me to perform a miracle,

    to manufacture a sign,
as if I was a soothsaying discloser
    of wondrous things.

Within his own sanctum,
    nearer than the jugular vein,
amid the rapid, fleeting
    fluctuations of the heart,
the Real through whom creation occurs

discloses Herself
at every instant, would that he knew
    the realities of things.

Had I produced a sparrow, what then
    would he have requested?

I offered the youth a handful of sand
    I let slip through my fingers
and the youth from Bounān departed
    cursing, bemoaning his lot.

Would that he knew that each grain of sand
    is a storehouse of Signs
and Names of manifest traces of Her
    in the corporeal world.

In the cosmos, every *thing* is an isthmus
    between two things,
sharing the attributes of both—
    the luminous and the corporeal.

Each Sign maps out algorithms
    of the Divine Womb
that lead to where the two seas meet
    but never mingle.

Revel in the Knowledge
    of the wondrous Names of our Creator
that share in the glory of oneness and many-ness
    all at once.

They name the one and only Real,
    representing the faces
of Her in the multifarious domain
    of Her Creation.

≈≈≈≈≈≈≈

It behooves wayfarers not to forget
    that wheresoever they turn,
they'll find Her face staring right at them
    for Her face is many-ness itself,
sourced from the spring
    of Her incontrovertible Oneness.

But the Real through whom
    creation occurs
has revealed to us
    that oneness preceded many-ness
in the cosmogony of Being—
    for without Being, the many
categorically could not exist—
    much like light preceded color,
        and mercy
      preceded wrath.

Know the realities of the One/Many
    and your place between them.

≈≈≈≈≈≈≈≈

As the intense angelic light disperses,
    boundlessly differentiating
the sensory temporal-spatial extension
    that is our own existence,
the isthmus continues to expand.

Within these borderlines, our soul
    may lean and amble
as it desires between the abodes
    of mercy and ignorance.

≈≈≈≈≈≈≈≈

'But what do you see there?'

asked another youth from Qaws,
thinking the isthmus is a place of wonders
    for eyes to behold
when it is the domain
    of the third eye alone.
How difficult it is to describe
    the indescribable!

Out of fear of discouraging the youth,
    I hesitantly revealed
how its canopying sky is a shade
    that is itself a cipher,
a color that is a meeting point
    between light and dark.

Its panoply of lunar bodies
    not only occupies the empyrean
but hangs and rotates in the æther
    within touching distance.

The soil is rich and oversaturated
    with every mineral
and can be fashioned like clay,
    breathed into and brought to life.

The wine-dark waters of the isthmian realm
    are undisturbed by even the slightest breeze.

Below the surface
    are untold mysteries
of the realities of things that somehow exist
    without agitating the still waters.

≈≈≈≈≈≈≈≈

'And what of the entities
    that populate the isthmus?'

What could I have possibly said
    other than: it is the domain
of corporeous entities and spirits
    of varied subtlety, of jinn
made of smokeless fire,
    who occupy the in-between by merit,
for they—much like our selves—are creatures
    burdened with free will.

There are the spirits of martyrs
    like Zāhira of Qurṭub,
Ṭāhā the Shepherd, Sayf of Erbā
    and Qamar of Maysawayn,
who sowed what was good,
    and whose bodies perished,
but whose souls did reap the rewards
    of the here, the in-between
and the hereafter.

      There are the spirits
    of eternal flame, who exalt unceasingly,
whose roles in the arc of creation
    are precalculated, who take the form
of celestial and physical bodies
    that follow Her designs.

Equally are they the souls
    of the fauna and flora
as they are the souls
    of Andromeda and Nebula
as they are the souls
    of the constellation clusters
as they are the souls
    of careering gaseous orbs
as they are the souls
    of oceans and their contents

as they are the souls
    of stars and their stuff,
and the souls of suns, moons
    and their stuff too.

≋≋≋≋

The beings of Light—the arwāḥ
    and other malāʾika—
they come and go as they please,
    for their presence
preceded created things
    in the supreme cosmogony.

They float freely and ride
    in horseless chariots
through the air, over the waters
    and across the planes,
moving effortlessly by the will
    of the Unmoved Mover.

Not only are they the couriers
    of the divine Reality,
but also the escorts
    of the prophets who came before,
who were themselves the couriers
    of the supreme Logos.

They exist eternally, entering
    and exiting the isthmus freely.

When the Merciful—
    who is also the Wise
and Utmost Real—
    disclosed Herself to them,

She did so in the tongue

of their communities,
that the discourse of the Supreme Reality
    be clear to them.

May their reward from the Merciful
    be exceedingly bounteous,
for theirs was a sacrifice
    not one of them desired,
for they feared rejection
    from their own kin,

and when indeed they faced persecution
    or were exiled,
they remained steadfast
    in their prophetic mission.

≈≈≈≈≈≈≈≈

O peace be upon the busy hands
    and callused soles
of the prophet Nūr of Qunayṭara,
    whose luminescence
filled the hearts
    and homes of her brethren,
empowering those who were made
    to feel powerless,
emancipating others by her effect
    on the fragile ego,
and loosening pride's grip on those
    willing to self-deprecate.

She brought them the Word
    and brought them a warning
of men who wreaked havoc
    and sowed discord in the Earth
and in the soil of their being,

which they heeded not.

O peace be upon the busy hands
    and callused soles
of the prophet Rakkān of Jawāzayn,
    whose wisdom
increased his community in knowledge
    of the Alive,
unfurling revelation rarefied
    rich and mellifluous,

yet their hearts did not easily accept
    the Word as did their ears,
for in their hearts was a sickness
    and She increased them in that sickness,
for they failed to realize
    their own wickedness,

    and when they burned at the stake
the messenger of the Possessor
    of the Day of Judgment,
the prophet from Jawāzayn
    gave a final warning
of the imminence of that Hour,
    which they heeded not.

O peace be upon the busy hands
    and callused soles
of the prophet Shams of Mādaba,
    who turned the tombs
of martyrs into shrines
    and turned the shrines of tyrants
into tombs unfit for the living,
    for the whisperer within
brought destruction to their empires
    and their communities.

When the prophet appeared to them
    with the Truth from the One
Who Takes Account of All Matters,

    they crucified Shams,
inverted his body, nailed him to the cross
    and left him to rot on the Eastern Road
between Jarash and Sufahān.

Yet the prophet from Mādaba
    felt not a thing, for his soul
had lifted from its shell
    and rose upright
from the world of bodies
    through the heavenly stations
to the Station of Proximity
    where it would find peace
in the Garden of Many Waters,
    from which the crucifiers will be refused,
for they received the Truth
    from the Sublime Witness,
        and paid no heed whatever.

O peace be upon the busy hands
    and callused soles
of the prophet Asyā of Tāshīn,
    servant of the Sovereign,
whose branded hands bore
    the mark of servitude
and whose beauty caught the eye
    of the tyrant of Azrā Kāf.

Unfailingly, she served none other than
    the Hearer of Invocation
who spoke to Her servant by way
    of the simurġh and the bee,
        in the language

of archetypes.

They disclosed to Asyā the mysteries
    of the supernal dominion
and warned her of the perilous realities
    of her prophetic mission.

Verily did the prophet of Tāshīn
    accept her fate,
and verily was she delivered
    by her beneficent Creator.

And when she returned
    to face the tyrant of Azrā Kāf,
demanding in the name of the Possessor
    of the Day of Judgment
the emancipation
    of her down-pressed kin,
        they fed her to the fire.

    But the Unfailing for her sake
made the fire cool and soothing,
    and when Asyā spoke from the flames
the tyrant of Azrā Kāf and his retinue
    prostrated themselves before her
and begged her to intercede on their behalf,
    lest they experience the true Fire.

These rightly guided prophets
    and thousands more freely access
whichever celestial abode they desire,
    once they've decoded every latent cipher,
thereby unlocking all the Knowledge
        that abode contains.

≈≈≈≈≈≈≈≈

When the youth from Qaws
    asked me how to meet them
on those shores,
    I offered him a mustard seed.
He levelled curses, crawled back
    into himself and departed.

Had he stayed a little longer,
    I would have divulged
that the gateway to the isthmus
    is through the imagination,
for the isthmus is in reality
    the imaginal realm, through which
we may ascend to the world of spirits
    and through which the world of spirits
may descend to us.
    Thus, it is the confluence
        for beings of all stations.

The mechanistic imagination
    is nothing but a tool,
whereas the imaginal world
    is both spatial and temporal,
but with space and Time utterly
    ungoverned by limitations,
where strictly metaphysical faculties
        are of any use at all.

Call the isthmus what you will:
    the imaginal world
is nondelimited and contains
    the totality of hierarchies,
where every impossibility is possible,
    and where contraries
come together and engage
    with every other possible thing.

The utterly nondelimited nature
    of the imaginal realm
makes it the most obvious plane
    of reality for the Real
to penetrate and disclose
        Herself.

Is She not nearer to us
    than our jugular veins?
How easy it is for Her to come to us,
    and would that we knew it,
how easy it is to come to Her,
    whether we are awake or asleep.

When we are truly awake,
    we are granted unique access
to that aqueous, dreamlike reality
    between two seas
where we are free to communicate
    with spirits, prophets and messengers,

free to ponder on the isthmian shores
    in wonderment,

free to interpret the traces
    of Her Names in all things,

free to produce paradisal fauna
    from the clay,

free to forfeit oneself to the peace
    of ungoverned eons,

free to witness but also touch
    the lunar and solar bodies,
and to understand
    their pregnant signs and ciphers.

In the great hierarchy of being,
    the imaginal mundus is She/not She—
Real, but not Real—neither this
    nor that—both this
and that; a realm of intrinsic ambiguity,
    where everything is annihilated
except the true faces of things,
    for the face of a thing
is its true nature.

    Wheresoever we turn,
whether in the realm of bodies
    or in the realm of spirits,
we testify to what we witness
    as we commingle between
        the realities
            of She/not She.

Part II
From *The Blue Dīwān*
Dīwān al-Azraq

Maxims

I

The sage who seeks
   will find.
The saint who knocks
   will have it opened.

II

The seeker who comes to know
   the world will find a corpse.
The seeker who finds a corpse
   is unworthy of either world.

III

The posturer who knows the One
   but in himself is lacking,
lacks everything
   and knows nothing.

IV

When the mystery of one becoming two
   at last is understood,
the child shall not resist separation
   from her mother's breast.

V

She lends her milk to suckling baby
    interest free.
Better to lend to whom you know
    cannot pay you back in kind.

VI

When brother and sister make peace
    with one another in a single house,
they will go to the mountain and shout,
    'Move from here!' and it will move.

VII

Remove the log that is in your eye
    so that you may remove
the speck that is in your sister's eye
    and the dirt in your brother's mouth.

VIII

And if light enters, and your being
    is stubborn and opaque,
remember that the Hearer of Invocation
    is also the Debaser, the Humiliator.

IX

A man gave Lūzān the messenger a coin,
    saying, 'The Paterōn demands his taxes,'
to which Lūzān replied, 'Give to the Paterōn what is his,
    what is Hers to Her, and what is mine, give to me.'

X

Worthy of anointment is the one
    who knows the precise hour
the robbers will enter—who rises early,
    musters her estate, and arms herself.

XI

The prostrate wayfarer drinks from the mouth
    and lo! becomes the river.
It is better to drown than to wade through mud
    in search of costly things.

XII

And the Real said, 'You assess the Earth
    and skies above, yet you've not come to know
the ones who came before, and know not
    how to assess the radical now.'

XIII

And she said, 'Direct my kin to divide
    my father's estate with me.'
And the Sovereign replied, saying, 'I will destroy
    your house and your father's estate.'

XIV

The primordial waters on which
    the ferryman plies his trade
swallow all the same
    those of high and low stations.

XV

The station of no-station is like a farm
    with hidden treasures buried in its fields
waiting for a drunk ploughman
    to bury his dead.

XVI

Sow seed and watch the fig trees
    grow beyond the planes.
Sow discord and lament the fruit
    while you feast on rotting bark.

XVII

When a shepherd with a flock of one hundred
    lost his largest sheep,
he left behind the ninety-nine and found the one
    saying to it, 'I love you more than them.'

XVIII

Woes betide the hordes who sow discord
    in the Earth, like wolves
sleeping in the cattle's feeding trough
    eating nothing, starving others.

XIX

Do not give dogs holy things
    lest they toss them to the dung heap.
Do not give swine precious jewels
    lest they grind them down.

XX

The sphere of smokeless fire is like a man
    who aimed to slay a dignitary, who stuck his blade
in the wall to make sure his hand would be firm,
    then murdered the dignitary.

XXI

The suitors who stand and wait at the door
    are many, though what's the use?
Only the eunuchs are allowed access
    to the bridal chamber.

XXII

When you're invited to the table,
    avoid the prominent seat,
for someone more prominent will enter,
    and the host will say, 'Go down lower!'

XXIII

and shame will be heaped on you.
    Better to pick the lowest seat.
The host will tell you to 'Come up higher!'
    and it will be you who benefits.

XXIV

Keep the cupbearer's hands busy
    and flatter them before the host.
Just remember that it is the sandal-bearer
    who is tasked with seeing you out.

XXV

The road to the Citadel hears prayers
    of pilgrims from every tribe.
Do not return after twelve years and say,
    'I did not hear them.'

XXVI

When flesh is found longing for the soul,
    and the soul for flesh,
the physician will find collyrium
    to salvage sight for the blind.

XXVII

Odious is the body
    that depends on a body,
and odious the soul
    that depends on the two.

XXVIII

The lion has its den, and the birds
    find shelter in their nest.
The thief will rue the fire and plead
    with bifurcated tongue.

XXIX

The one whose right hand conceals stones,
    their left hand will be given pearls.
The one with nothing in either hand
    will have an eye removed.

XXX

No servant can serve two masters
    in a single house.
They exalt the one
    and insult the other—

XXXI

a sycophant
    schismatic
mounting two horses,
    stringing two bows.

XXXII

The slavedriver builds his high castle
    on the mountain top
so fortified, it cannot fall.
    It cannot hide either.

XXXIII

A prophet was never welcome
    in her own community.
Those whose lips recite her revelation
    will meet a rare demise.

XXXIV

The paradisal pastures and the Earth
    shall furl before the folk of the evident Reality
who've tasted death's incarnate fruit
    and lived.

XXXV

Go ask a sage,
   'What is it like in the afterlife?'
If they do not hand you a mustard seed,
   they're no sage at all.

XXXVI

A true disciple, much like
   the asphodel tree of paradise,
blossoms just the same in summer,
   autumn, winter, and spring.

XXXVII

Yet you persist by asking,
   'How will my end come about?'
How does one seek the end
   if they have yet to find the beginning?

XXXVIII

And the Sovereign said, 'Come to me,
   for my yoke is easy, and my rule is kind.
Come to me, and you will find
   repose.'

XXXIX

And She said, 'The one who is near Me
   is near the Fire,
and the one who is far from Me is far
   from the pleroma.'

XL

Seek the flame, split the wood,
    leave not a stone unturned.
Wheresoever you cast a combing eye,
    you'll find Her there.

XLI

When you see your likeness,
    you are jubilant.
But when you see what came before—
    pre-eternal and unmanifest—what then?

XLII

Her imperishable aspects
    will be unveiled to you,
and the darkness they dispel
    shall be dissolved.

XLIII

It is easy enough to know all there is
    and believe you've gained.
It is something else to find the Self
    and gain nothing whatsoever.

XLIV

And Sākina responded, 'You asked for things
    I withheld from you before.
Now I am willing to disclose all things
    and you no longer ask for them.'

XLV

Go find the rejected cornerstone
    and from it build a home.
Lapis lazuli, silver and gold
    befit the funeral pyre.

XLVI

The sandal-bearer carries with her
    the mysteries in the day
and in the night rehearses her salutations
    for the ferryman.

XLVII

Even as the twilight hours approach,
    seek out the living.
It is good to serenade the ferryman
    on your night-journey.

XLVIII

Envy those who have suffered,
    and from their suffering found life.
The ferryman relishes those who find life
    in the suffering of others.

XLIX

When the ferryman asks,
    'Where exactly are you coming from?'
do not reply by asking,
    'Where exactly are you taking me?'

A. A. Telmesani

L

Instead, tell the ferryman that you've come
   from the land of the dead
and he will gladly ferry you in speed
   to the land of the living.

Lo, in the Month
of Ḏhul Qiʿdah

Simurġh, what course are we set
    to commence when the Hour arrives?

All of Creation depends on the whim
    of the Fashioner's Calamus
sprung from the void of supernal infinity,
    timeless, beginningless,
out from behind the æthereal veil
    that divides the dimensional
planes of both subtle and bodily beings.

Song most sublime! O Muse of the Real!
    Give us a sign of your Master's devices,
        lest we be the ones
    who move blindly in ignorance.

O, in the name of the Merciful Real
    through whom all creation occurs,

Light of the East and the West,
    unique among noblest of Lords—

Possessor of Names set in stone
    at the base of Her holiest tree—

the banyan of banyans long gracing
    the sanctum sanctorum of eons flown by.

Prophets whose right-guided footsteps
    led millions of road-weary novices
out of the shadows and onto the virtuous

path of the wayfaring
courtesans destined to sit at the foot
    of the Merciful Advocate—
fated to feel the soft hem of Her garment
    of rarefied axial Light.

They are the ones who possess
    the sound knowledge bestowed
by the Hearer, the Ever-Relenting,
    preeminent Master of Time.

    Spirits and entities, they all bent willfully—
dæmons unholy and angels
    of purely essential nobility—
when the good news was sent forth from on high,
    when the Aleph obediently cried,
releasing the Letters and Names
    from their mansions sublime.

Even the Paterōn's famous diviners
    debased themselves utterly
under the weight of Her aegis as surely
    as dew dangles happily
evening through morn on the delicate branches
    and leaves, when the heralding
sun rides her chariot forth from beneath
    the horizon all-conquering.

Source of all sources, the oceans
    would readily dry, and the skies
would cleave open ere even a word
    that describes Your true eminence
ever rang out.
    At the Reckoning Hour,
Ursā shall blow her all-conquering trumpet
    to gather the multitudes
when they shall face the malāʾika

        waiting to use
their own words to deny them
        safe passage to Jannā's lush gardens
with liquid light well-springs
        and pleasure domes teeming
with prophets engaged in decoding
        the signs of their Sovereign.

Part III
From *Carmina Terræ*
Aġhānil Arḍ

Safāw

O Mover, who moves the heavenly bodies
    and turns the constellations and brings forth
the seasons—see how the soothsayers calculate
    and extrapolate wise and ill-fated portents
from the same spheres and astral bodies
      as those that guide the seekers and astronomers,
        whose charts map out
      the Auroræ and the Northern Lights.

O Mover of the supernal spheres,
    unleash Your designs! Kāf—the Palm
of the Pleiades, Dābiḥ—the Slaughterer's
    Lucky Star, Kalburrāi—The Shepherd's Dog,

      Gumaesā—the Bleary-Eyed, Janāḥ—
Orion's Wing, Rāsul Hamal—
    the Head of the Ram,

and every other gaseous orb
      blazing the courses
        of Your imagination.

See how Your stars burn out
    and expand the borderlines
of what is visible in the unpenetrated dark
    of the lower spheres,

whose sublime resplendence induced
    a theophanic flash of Self-disclosure so intense
that it snatched an illiterate orphan—
    a Kārūnite—from out her body
and into the archetypal world,

where æthereal beings greeted her
as if she too was made
    of light or smokeless fire.

She gazed in wonderment as she observed
    the isthmian shores for the first
       of many times.
And when the prophets, jinn, and malāʾika
    approached the illiterate orphan
and made her aware of her axial purpose,
    she professed to them her love
of verse-craft and the need for tutoring
    in the science of the Names and Letters.
She implored and offered herself to Elia
    of the malāʾika and begged the being of light
to instruct her, and to allow her access
    to the quintessence of Monadic gnosis.
She did this in the presence
    of the prophets and messengers
who witnessed her initiation
    and Elia's bestowal of the mantle
       of the First Intellect

    when she was then returned to her body
back in the world of engendered things
    by Rāfa the Charioteer in the dead of night
who thereafter carried her in his horseless
    wingèd car as she soundly slept
and left her at the calligrapher's doorstep.

    O Mover, see how she awoke
to the sound of Your whispering:

    'O Ḥafsa! which of My signs
       do you deny?'

O Mover, see how Ḥafsa was reduced to tears
    at the feet of Your servant, the calligrapher,
and how he taught her to hold the calamus
    and guided her hand and taught her
the science of the Names and Letters.
    See how she excelled in her discipline
and advanced in her rhetorical
    and prosodic skills under his guidance
and how she learned the ways
    of the Eloquent Creator
and the Preserved Tablet.
    See how Ḥafsa devoted herself to him
as his apprentice, and aided him
    as the agèd man's sight began to fail.

And on the calamitous day that she lost
    her beloved master, and she was orphaned
once again, see how she sat daily
    by a well with a begging bowl
waiting for merchants and pilgrims
    to pass her by, to whom she could recite
her craftily improvised qaṣa'id and zajal,
    and see how briskly they retreated
        when they did,
    avoiding eye contact at all costs.

O Mover, see how You compel the courses
    of fate and the heartstrings of human beings!
See how Ḥafsa halted and moved an envoy one night
    to tears as they walked by and heard her reciting
poems from her storehouse, who then begged her
        to accompany them to Heliopolis.

See how Ḥafsa was received
    by the Regina Materōn, who made Ḥafsa
perform a recitation that slew her entire retinue.

See how Ḥafsa was placed on a scale
and was offered her weight in pure gold,
    an entourage of houri boys
        and other fineries.

O Mover, see how your movements
    direct the courses of the spheres and the galaxies
as well as the course of an illiterate orphan
    snatched out of her body by Your will
and lifted from the station of poverty to the ranks
    of imperial poet-laureate and esteemed courtier.

≈≈≈≈≈≈≈≈

O Nourisher, what the Safāw lacks in sweet well-water,
the pristine, mineral-rich streams of the Zāgra
    that fall from the paradisal peaks of Anbūr
        provide in abundance.

O Nourisher, songbirds take flight and fill the ears
    of the ploughmen and the herders and the pickers
and the millers and the brewers and the bakers,
    who in turn satiate the bodies of lutenists and lyric poets
whose souls are in turn snatched from their bodies like Ḥafsa
    and whose songs are transmitted by wayfarers
        in caravans crossing the Safāw.

O Nourisher, see how the olive groves of Āpilāi,
neither of the East nor of the West, produce nectar
    that lights the way for the night-clad pilgrim trains,
and how they provide fruit for the traveling company
    in the light of day.

O Nourisher, see how the Zāgra inundates
the floodplains, removing all traces of fields
    of wheat and corn and sorghum and sugar cane
and how it recedes in time for Safāwans to till,

sow seed, implore Gāiā, watch them sprout,
    take root, and rise from the ground for harvest
      before the Zāgra inundates once more
        and destroys it all again.

O Nourisher, when the Safāw
    suffers drought, You bring down rain.
When the plains are crusted with ice
    through early spring, Your sun,
like a charioteer on her return
    from some far-away campaign,
brings relief to Your people.

≈≈≈≈≈≈≈≈

O Fashioner, see how You, at every instant,
    fashion anew each blade and tendril,
each mineral, each sulfurous grain of Earth,
    each wind-swept carpel, dancing petal,
scattered sepal, each stamin
    tossed by the western zephyr.

See how You fashioned the reed beds
    of the wetlands, as well as the hands of Zakarāi
son of Marzamā of the clan of Ḥukk
    of the ancient city of Āpilāi, who cut
and fashioned a reed into an instrument
    fit for the Fashioner of spheres
whose breath produced a timbre
    so rich, it even slew the heretic
zealots who profane unrelentingly
      the Master Musician —
      the Real
who fashioned the degrees of the scales,
    and their tempered modes
that were then unerringly arranged

by Zakarāi—the righteous
stalwart of the gathering lights
   and their presences—son of Marzamā.

O Fashioner, when a reed in the wetlands
     laments its loneliness
and yearns for a mate, you send an outcast
   bursting at the seams, O Fashioner,
with the unceasing torrent of archetypes,
   yearning for a means to express them.

When the reed and outcast commiserated
   over the degrees of their loneliness,
You relieved them of their burden
   through the shared act of creation,
consummating musician and instrument.

Zakarāi made manifest the essences
   of the perfect and imperfect intervals
and strung them one by one,
   pearl by pearl, note by note, into melodies
tailor-made for Monadic Formulæ.
   See how those melodies sore
and lilt in the cantos of congregants
   in the temples of Āpilāi.

O Zakarāi son of Marzamā,
   see how your inventions
and Forms made their way
   through your being, your body,
 to the tip of your tongue—
   how your technique
produced such a pure sound
   by your breathing into the Fashioner's
reed-flute, and how that sound travelled
   in the chants of wayfarers
and their caravans across the Zāgra

along the silk and amber roads stretching
from the Ṭā'ifā Plateau to Gālibūr,
    from the Delta to the Great Stone Hall
of Martyrs in the Temple of No Station.

    See how the son of Marzamā's music
is now ubiquitous, and is heard
    in the songs of supplicants
and used to ornament and glorify
    the psalms and their hymnals,
that they too may recognize
        the mysteries therein.

O Fashioner, who fashions *ex nihilo*
    the subtle and substantial
by commingling disparate parts
    from the cloud of chaos,

who fashions the fleeting Forms
    imagined in the isthmus
between the worlds of corporeal
    and corporeous beings,
who fashions the shores
    on which they meet,

who fashions their speech
    from the cloth of pre-eternal
archetypes, who unceasingly
    fashions dwellings for beasts
of all nations, and who fashions their demise
    through calculated machinations—

to You belong the fates of empires—
    the Heliopolite, the Hittite,
The Turkānid, and Echæmenid—
    and of the clans and tribes
of Kāyā and Kashātra—city-states hell-bent

on annihilating the other
through cyclical blood-feuds
    unchecked,
entirely ignorant of Your
    prescriptive Command.

≈≈≈≈≈≈≈≈

O Slayer, who slew the phalanxes of Iskandar,
    who dismantled their chariots,
who separated and split their wheels
    and launched their drivers
        into the air,
who rained upon their cavalry
    arrows that blotted out the sun,
who let loose the spears
    that pierced their chests
and smashed their skulls,

who abased the high
    and cut down the low,
who soaked the Safāw
    with the blood of millions
from the age of ignorance
    to the founding of the City—
verily, it is You, O Slayer,
    who scattered their entrails
and their dismembered corpses
    and offered with great generosity
their rotting flesh to Gāiā
    and all her children
        who roam the Earth.

How easily you swallow
    whole armies!
O Slayer,

debaser of men.

≈≈≈≈≈≈≈

O Bringer of Reckoning, when the tyrant
    Yāsiq of Karak—oppressor, butcher
and violator of Safāwan people—
    cleansed Kārūn and Ramz
of all Gāiān men,
        and raped, enslaved,
    and mutilated
        all Gāiān women,
and burned their holy texts
    and quartered all of those
caught whispering recitations
    from their gnostic scrolls—
did they not realize that You
    are the ultimate Reckoner?

When Kārūn and Ramz entreated the aid
    of the clans of Dārwāsīn in the East
and the clans of Yusrāw in the West
    and their forces descended upon the citadel
and the citizens of Ramz joined their allies
    in storming the stronghold, when they blocked
all entryways and went from room to room,
    when they tracked Yāsiq down
like a pack of wolves and captured him,
    and dragged him from the watchtower
down to the central square,
    erected gallows, and read his crimes aloud,
and delivered his verdict
    to the liberated people of Ramz,
did he forget that not one soul—
    no sandal-bearer, slave, tyrant or lord—
        escapes Your reckoning?

And when the Hittite
   reign of terror consumed the peoples
of the border lands of Safāw and Gālibūr,
      and the western zephyr met
with the eastern stream in collaboration
   with the peoples of Danā᾽, Zabāt, Minyā,
and Kunaytara—whose communities were crushed
   by the weight of tyranny and the erasure
of their shared religions and cultural heritages—
   when they plotted patiently, clandestinely,
      to take back their ancient citadel,
   their Gāiān meeting houses,
and their great libraries and academies
   that their Hittite overlords laid to waste,

   the beings of light and fire cried out
and Gāiā's Earth yawned
   in preparation for the feast.

When the hour fell, wave after wave
   of border folk flared, and Hittite necks
received the lusting onslaught
   of Danā᾽ steel, Kunaytara bronze,
and Minyā iron with the fury and force
   of fifty years of plotting.

As their heads flew
   and their skulls were crushed,
and as life-breaths slipped away
   and as eyes bid farewell
to the gift of sight, and as gored,
   truncated carcasses fell as carrion—
did they not realize that You
   are the ultimate Truncator of life-breaths,
      bodies and reigns of terror,
         O Bringer of Reckoning?

A. A. Telmesani

≈≈≈≈≈≈≈

O Determiner, the poets of Safāw,
    of Kārūn and Adāi all commemorate
the Day of the Genocide at every harvest feast
    lest we forget our own capacities as humans
to commit heinous acts against one another.

        It was on the first of Rajab
in the dead of night when Fāris᾽ fanatical mercenaries
    loosed the first projectiles that smashed
into Adāi's obsidian gates. West of the city,
    his forces built a pontoon bridge that allowed
their colossal war engines—their trebuchets,
    siege towers and battering rams—to thunder across
            the Zāgra River effortlessly
                and with impunity.

The walls surrounding the city were high,
    but they were ancient, and fragile
in the face of fiery missiles
    the size of houses that rained down
and razed them asunder.

    When the siege towers were within
three-bow's distance, their drawbridges
    were deployed, and long-swordsmen
streamed onto the parapets
    and cut down Adāi's archers
with a merciless, fanatical lust
        devoid of pity.

    Within a few hours, before the sun
reached its zenith, Adāi's western walls
    were laid to waste and the city breached.

In the catastrophe that ensued,
   when the fanatical mercenary forces flooded
into Adāi freely, fleeing mothers and fathers—
   fully aware of the reputations
of Fāris and his mercenaries—resorted
   to either drowning their children
in wells or tossing them, then themselves,
   off the highest reachable rooftop or parapet,
that they might enjoy a more merciful,
     less humiliating end.

   All Gāiān women and girls
were raped, mutilated, and enslaved
   while all Gāiān males were rounded up
in the public square and in large, successive waves,
   were either immolated, beheaded, or crucified,
     beginning with the children,
       then the men.

When the slaughter began, it did not stem
   or cease until the square was awash
with Gāiān blood and the stench
   of burning corpses thickened the air.

But O Determiner, how the people of Adāi
   sought vengeance upon Fāris of Azrā Kāf
and his hordes, for it was You who gathered
   the nations of the floodplains
on either side of the Zāgra—of Rāi, of Kāyā,
   and Wādiram of the West Delta—
fierce nemeses of old—of Marsalām and Mādaba,
   who converged on Adāi with three hundred
thousand cavalrymen, infantrymen, charioteers,
   archers and a fleet of war engines;
and it was You, O Determiner, who determined
   the glorious hour, when at last, on the fourteenth day

of the month of Rajab, in an assault
    that lasted mere hours,
      Adāi was taken back;
  and it was You who determined
the uncompromising fate and adjudication
    that the elders of Adāi meted out upon the cruel,
rapacious hordes of Fāris of Azrā Kāf,
    who did not realize that You
        are the Determiner
    and ultimate Adjudicator
        of men.

In the days that followed the retaking of the city,
Fāris of Azrā Kāf was disemboweled
    and hung by his entrails from the western gate.

      As for the rest,
the most fortunate of his mercenaries were enslaved,
    while those guilty of the most heinous acts
were vertically cleaved in half or beheaded
    while the remnant troops were crucified upside down,
and their crosses fixed along the western banks
    of the delta.

  Their inverted, rotting corpses
dotted the amber road for miles—
    from Adāi all the way to Marsalām.

Thus was recorded by the poets of Safāw,
    of Kārūn and Adāi.

≈≈≈≈≈≈≈≈

O Abundant One—see how You made abundant
    the fruit of the Cerulean, and made abundant
the means of feeding, trading, and prospering
    on its abundance, and made abundant

the influx of goods from exotic lands—
    silks, spices, gems, jewels, silver, gold,
        and other diverse fineries.

Those who traded also purveyed
    in sacred and profane knowledge
in the form of caches of codices innumerable
    and transcribed reports that circulated
and dazzled the minds, and challenged
    predispositions of Safāwans, who codified,
commented on and expanded the canon,
    synthesizing and harmonizing it
with their own systems—producing,
    over millennia, an abundance
of variant sects and schools of thought,
    thereby banishing all forms of ignorance
        from their lands with Your
            abundant Knowledge!

≈≈≈≈≈≈≈≈

O Multiplier, who brought multiplicity
    out from nonexistence after giving
the Command: *Be!*—when Oneness
    birthed Twoness, birthed Threeness,
birthed Fourness, birthed Fiveness,
        unto infinity.

O Multiplier, through whom creation multiplies
    unceasingly at every instant,
from Form to Form,
        ever multiplying.

O Multiplier, who multiplies careering orbs
    and suns, see how the fauna graze
and multiply, how predators prey
    and multiply, and the people who share

the plains of Safāw with them,
>how they breed
>>and multiply.

O Multiplier, whose manifest Signs
>include the predators who consume gazelle,
ibex, red, fallow, and roe deer, who graze
>and multiply across the plains,
from Anbūr to the sea, from Hazar
>to the River Zāgra, from the Upper Valley
>>to the Lower.

O Multiplier, see how the people of Safāw
>make use of their oxes, mules, elephants,
camels, and free-roaming wild horses.

>See how they breed and raise cattle
that multiply, and how they slaughter,
>consume,
>>and multiply.

≈≈≈≈≈≈≈

O Unifier, how supremely privileged
>are the people of Safāw,
the custodians of Heliopolis—City of the Sun—
>the Founded City—the very heart
of the Zāgra Valley and throne
>of Earthly power!

O Unifier, who made hallow its grounds,
>and established its Grand Sanctuary
as the nexus of pilgrimage for pilgrims
>of every creed and calling—truly You
are the Unifier of all peoples, races,
>religions and variant sects.

≈≈≈≈≈≈≈

Guarding the western front
    is holy Mount Hazar—
locus of the Final Hour—
    Time's burial ground.

To the South, in the Upper Valley,
    springs the fount of the Alive—
the life-begetting River Zāgra
    that flows from the peaks
        of Mount Anbūr,

and to the North, in the Lower Valley,
    gapes the mouth of the Delta,
where the Zāgra consummates her journey
    and merges into the Cerulean.

O Unifier, from Hazar to Heliopolis,
    from Anbūr to the sea,
how supremely privileged are the people
    of Safāw! who exhibit equal
and unqualified amnesty toward refugee
    philosophers, exiles, and flower-eaters
        all the same.

O Unifier, was it not You who unified
    the clans of Katam, and the houses
of Yahzar and Qarbāya—the shared
    descendants of the martyred prophets
Edris Anṣār and Ushbihān
    whose blood feuds raged
from one generation to the next,
    from the very first offense
in the late third century
    through the great drought of 397
that made fallow the floodplains
    west of the River Zāgra?

Was it not You who willed
    the indiscriminate raids
of the favored peoples and honored clans
    of Katam and Tāshīn, whose daughters
and sons were ambushed,
    kidnapped and held for ransom
in a time of dire poverty
    that led to untold savageries
in an unending cycle
    of genocidal retribution?

And was it not You, O Unifier, who sent
    the noble prophet Waisāʾ — daughter
of Turāwah of the Munirites — to warn
    of the impending storm of the marauders
of Biyahmu?
                Was it not You who gathered
    the two warring houses of Katam and Tāshīn,
and united them in the great alliance
    that repelled the armies of Kāzā Ghayn
            and ended their reign
                of terror on the plains?

    Verily, it is You, O Unifier, who sets the scales
and demarcates the two unmingling seas
    and makes subtle the isthmian veils,
and purifies the souls of axial saints,
    and ennobles and raises them on high,
like Waisāʾ the Munirite, who ended all hostilities
    and unified the tribes of Katam and Tāshīn
and Ramz and Kārūn and Buyūtāt and Sāḍḍ,
    and who unveiled to them the mysteries
        of Your vast panoplies
            in the Kūfic tongue
        that Your Word be clear to them,
                O Unifier.

Dārwāsīn

145

I

If I had to retrace Gāiā's steps,
    where else would I start but Dārwāsīn?
If I were asked a million times,
    a million times I would answer Dārwāsīn!

If I had to retrace Gāiā's steps,
    my animal self would roam unloosed
        the grasslands raging!

If I had to retrace Gāiā's steps,
    I would prostrate and study the ratios
and the subtleties of stem and stamen
    in measures both separate and equal.

If I had to retrace Gāiā's steps,
    I would infiltrate the herds
of gazelle and antelope.
    Even they move at the whim
of the Mover, who moves
    the heavenly bodies and the herds.

If I had to retrace Gāiā's steps,
    I would scour the grasslands
of Dārwāsīn in flight with fleet-
    footed foxes on the prowl.

If I had to retrace Gāiā's steps,
    I would place my ear to the ground
and follow the stampede of wild

elephants as they migrate
up and down the windy banks
    of the River Zāgra.

If I had to retrace Gāiā's steps,
    I would call upon the Bringer
of Seasons to turn the winter
    into spring in time to sow,
and on the Guarantor
    to guarantee an ample harvest.

Gāiā of the vast Earth! Gāiā skin,
    Gāiā bone, stuff of Gāiā! Root of Gāiā!
Stone Gāiā, mountain metal Gāiā,
    Gāiā Gargantua, sulphur Gāiā,
        on the plain Gāiā,
dune-shifting! Night and day Gāiā!
    Primeval Gāiā, tufting,
        loose-dirted Gāiā,
grit-crunching Gāiā of mouthfuls!
    Gāiā meliora, festoon-rutted song of Gāiā,
milk and ghee-fat goated Gāiā!
    Hoof-hucked plenum of the grasslands!
Dragging feet dragging calamus
    drag of Gāiā! Cool water Gāiā!
        sweet, free-running,
to the briny firmament-fleshed
    Gāiā of the sea! We salute
        the rogue queen: Gāiā
            of the teeming Dārwāsīn.

    Dārwāsīn, the well-endowed,
gushing land of o'erspread bodies.
    Dārwāsīn, the doctrinal seat of creeds
that raised on high the houses.
    Dārwāsīn, the overflowing well-spring

of unrepeating archetypes.
   Dārwāsīn, the guttural, rasping,
sun-choked breath of the Living,
   Dārwāsīn, the heaving and the hoe-ing
     waft of the animate dying!

Untamed panhandle of the bifurcating
   river-cradle of capitals;
Untamed arbitrator of the blood-feuding
   lords of Buyutāt and Āpilāi;
Untamed child of equal parts fashioner
   and equal parts desecrator.

Untamed grassy pleroma unfurled
   by the Manifester of pleromas;
Untamed, uncured, unrinsed, unripe,
   gestating beast of gathering!

    II

When they say, 'How fine are the fineries
   of Dārwāsīn?' Howl from the parapets! and say
'Fine are the horn of plenty meeting houses;
   fine are the occupiers of their sweat-stained
pulpits that rain down missile prayers upon
   the noose-tight congregation; of game-house
chancers, snake-oil hawkers, and lame skin-walkers;
   of libertines and the spawn of libertines;
of celibates and the spawn of celibates;
   of hash mongers and the spawn of hash mongers;
whore-hounds and the spawn of whore-hounds;
   of invalids and the spawn of invalids;
of the soiled and the spawn of the soiled;
   of the raised on high and the spawn
of the raised on high; of the most abased
   and the spawn of the most abased;

of the regurgitators and the spawn of regurgitators;
   of the dirt eaters and the spawn of dirt eaters;
of the hog-sloppers and the spawn
   of hog-sloppers; of the soft-gutters
and the spawn of soft-gutters; of silk-wormers
   and the spawn of silk-wormers; of rakes
and the spawn of rakes; of barefoot sandal-bearers
   and the spawn of barefoot sandal-bearers;
of juveniles and the spawn of juveniles;
   of zealots and the spawn of zealots!

Foreigner, what do you know
   about congregations?

Fine are the stonecutters of Qishāra
   who hack whole cities out
      of the quarries of Anbūr.

Fine are the nomadic shepherds
   whose herds and flocks graze
in the foothills, and are grazed upon
      by foothill folk
   and the beyond-foothill folk.

Fine are the aṭṭārs of Dunyā, busy extracting musk
   from the glandular excretions of gazelles,
chameleons and crocodiles; extracting ambergris
   from the tracts of sperm, hump-back
and other fat fruit of the Cerulean;
      procuring myrrh, frankincense, labdanum,
         camphor and copaiba gum resin;
sapping aetheroleum of sassafras
   and cassia bark; of clove, hop,
hyssop, marjoram, manuka;
      of anise, flax and nutmeg, of cedar, agar,
         rose and sandalwood; of tea tree,
            melaleuca, and eucalyptus.

How busy are the hands
     of the aṭṭārs of Dunyā!

Fine are the glass-blowers busy blowing
     and staining macro and microcosms,
hylic wonders and spherical oddities,
     blowing and staining exquisite murals
of the sacred and the profane;
     blowing instruments for the physician
and the distiller and the astronomer
     and the diviner and the poppy-farmer
          and the navigator out at sea.

Fine are the tanners of Qishāra
     busy harvesting, curing, soaking, liming,
scudding, deliming, bating,
     drenching, pickling and finishing
their rawhides that keep warm kin
     and valley-folk alike.

Fine are the scribe novitiates of Buyutāt
     and their postulating pedagogues
syllogizing in the fora of their academies,
     keeping records of histories and treatises,
systematically collecting and copying
     folk anthologies and sacred texts and manuals
of the esoteric and exoteric sciences
     and preserving and cataloguing them
          in the great Library of Buyutāt.

Fine are their rhetoricians who spin their ways
     into the courts of regents, ladies, lords, Materōns
and Paterōns, who place them on scales
     and pay them their weight in gold to spin
sycophantisms at their whim and pleasure.

Fine are the singers and the pipers
   and the lutenists and the harpists
and the mizmārists and the reed-flautists
   and the gourd-banjoists and the lithophonists
and the lyrists and the bullroarers
   and the water organists and the conch shell
trumpeters and the metallophonists
   and the ocarinists and the qānūnists
and the rabābists and the kamānjanists
   of Buyutāt's grand conservatory
who pluck archetypes out of the æther
   and flood the air with free-floating traces
      of the myriad Names of the Emancipator.

Fine are the weavers of Qishāra who spin
   royal-purple brocade from the silk
of Yusrāwan silkworms and gold
   from the mines of the Ṭā'ifā Plateaus,
but who also spin frocks and tunics and cloaks
   and breeches and habits for the coarse,
carefree folk of Dārwāsīn who are truly
   the precious gem-and-metal boon
      of the Zāgra Valley.

Fine are the grammarians, linguists,
   philologists, and genealogists,
who track the ins and outs—the foreign,
   the domestic, the common, the exotic,
the banned and the permissible,
   the sound, the confuted, the plain,
the perfect, the imperfect, the pluperfect,
   the conjured, the ordinary and extraordinary,
the simple, the past and present participle,
   the future tense, the glottal and the palatal,
the vocalized, the unvocalized, the terse
   and the drawn out, the borrowed, the stolen,

the right way, the wrong way, the cursive,
    the discursive, the modified, the unmodified,
the living, the extinct, the obtuse, the acute,
        and the radicalized.

Fine are the artisans—the sculptors, engravers,
    silver, brass and copper-workers, potters,
jewelers, mandala mappers—whose hands
    move by the will of the Unmoved Mover,
whose creations usher from the fount
    of the Creator, whose surgical precision vies
with that of the heavenly bodies
    in their fixed courses back to the Real
through whom their creation occurred,
    whose kilns bake and double bake
earthenware for the homestead,
    bricks for the bricklayers, and canopic jars
        for the priests and the shamans.

Fine are Dārwāsīn's academies
    of secular and sacred sciences
at Jawāzayn and Buyutāt
    and Dunyā and Qishāra.

Fine are their mathematicians, engineers,
    astronomers, astrologers, architects,
calligraphers, cartographers, and fine
    are their women and men of letters
        at the zenith of their influence.

Fine are their vying schools of jurisprudence,
    and fine are their head-butting exegetes,
        compilers and traditionists.

Fine are the meeting houses and courtyards
    of the peripatetic schools, and fine
are their faculties of naturalists, rationalists,

logicians, rhetoricians, ethicists,
occultists, metaphysicians, cosmologists
    and numerologists.

       III

Ask me again, foreigner,
    of the fineries of Dārwāsīn.
But hear this time through the All-Hearing
    and behold through the All-Seeing.
And if you would speak,
    speak in the name of the Knowing,
and by the tongue of the Eloquent
    and the Sublime.
And when it is time to listen
    once more, reach inward
to the Tranquil and the Patient.
    Remember that the boundaries
of Dārwāsīn are a complete figment
    of your steadily-ripening
        imagination.

# Part IV
From *Chronicles*
Tawārīkh

Sanctum

I

In the name of the Real through whom
    Creation occurs, whose astral entities
follow Her precalculated designs,
    whose merciful breath brought forth
the Pen with 'Be!' and the preserved
    eternal tablet without beginning or end,
who caused the gaseous orbs to glorify
    Her Name along with every entified
existent coursing the empyrean,

    whose traces permeate the perfect pleroma
outspread, who made manifest the known
    unknown by sound decree and unfurled
the hierarchies and unveiled the stations
    and set them by rank degree of nearness
to Your Footstool, O Manifest Light Scatterer,
    Sovereign of the gathering Cry.

≈≈≈≈≈≈≈≈

A million moons ago, or so it seems,
    beneath the star of the great ʿanqāʾ,
a young girl slipped out in the night
    in the hours exclusive to rakish folk
and opium dens, racked by thoughts
    of unusual perplexity, impoverished
of spirit, desperate to know without knowing

154

the knowable unknown, thirsty to taste
the vintage of stone sages, anxious
    to grasp the realities of things
as they really are, lost in the wilderness,
    devoid of notions, uninclined toward
forethought, utterly impatient,
    a vacuous being yoked by impulse—
that rudderless fanatical charioteer.

    She knew not the hymns of the Names,
but was drawn from alley way to alley way,
    from street to street by the song of the zephyr
      of union and abandonment.

She crossed into the precinct
    of the holy sepulcher barefoot
in a state of ritual impurity, weaving
    her way through the honeycomb vaults
of the Grand Sanctuary, navigating
    the dense forest of inscribed columns
and into the sanctum sanctorum
    of the Great Banyan.

There, in the heart of the Holy House—
    that unique nexus and eye of the world
of bodies—in the hours of rakish folk
    and opium dens, the men of tasting—
guardians—or so they proclaimed—
    of the supernal pillars of natural
and sacred sciences held
    their nightly vigil
      out of earshot
     of patrolling zealots.

She feigned awareness of their intimate
    concatenations and made her feet busy,
infiltrating a train of lay pilgrims

circumambulating the Great Banyan—
themselves unaware of her scheming
    and using them for clandestine purposes.

How else would a fourteen-year-old
    go freely about her business?

'O to be a rakish man or opium addict,
    free to roam about!' she thought as she craned
her neck and stretched her ear toward the men
    of tasting as they syllogized
and interpreted scripture.
    She strained to hear each syllable
as she slowly circumambulated the Great Banyan.

For hours on end, she drank up ciphers
    from the ambrosial fount of these traffickers
of mysterious and wondrous panoplies,
    of what she would not know for many years
to be anything other than sempiternal theophanies
    that freely rained down on the prepared hearts
        of saints and seekers of pure gnosis.

    Of course, she knew nothing of these orders
of infinity, these subtle Self-disclosures
    ushered from the merciful Breath
directly into the ears of Her most
        impoverished confidants.

Each fragmented cipher that caught
    in her throat on its way into her lungs
and bloodstream on route to the heart
    was nothing other than that: a cipher—
a veil obstructing entry into the abode
    of many waters, verdant vistas
        and unspoken Vast Earth alchemy.

Each cipher she consumed was a dazzling
    yet isolated Form stripped from a tapestry
of equally dazzling, spellbinding Forms,
    that, as she contemplated them, produced
a drunkenness fit for honored patrons
    of late-night taverns and gaming houses.

    Each tattered strip of confounding gnosis
left her stupefied, as the shoreless ocean
    of divine cognition swallowed her.

Only when the men of tasting
    with their divine ciphers retired
following the dawn vigil
    did she manage to stumble home
to a mother who beat her senseless
    to the point of exhaustion.

And yet she persisted daily,
    as if her nightly obfuscations
to the Sanctuary to eavesdrop
    uncracked ciphers somehow
alchemically healed her unsightly
        bodily injuries.

And when this child grew tired
    of delinquent eavesdropping,
she threw the dice of fate and sat
    among these men of tasting,
who proceeded to chastise
    and threaten her with violence
then banished her from their intimate
    gathering place. They hurled a hail
        of projectiles at her
            as she fled the scene.

'O to be among the rakes and addicts
    free to roam about!' she lamented
as she licked her wounds and sobered up
    from drinking unchecked quantities
        of gnostic-grade vintage.

She forlornly ambled through
    the bustling alleyways
as the witching hour approached,
    when no-goodness reigned.

But the hazy plumes from the opium dens
    would soon scatter, and the sounds
of revery would be replaced with the sounds
    of semi-lucid, drunk penitents
rushing home in shame, and the clattering
    carts and epithets of yawping vendors vying
        for premium thoroughfare.

As she weaved her way back home,
    consumed by despair
and overwhelmed by the feeling of rejection,
    the miserable child wept so profusely
that she had very few tears left to shed
    when confronted with battery
        as she entered her front door.

II

That very evening, undeterred,
    she cut her flowing locks,
wrapped her bosom tight
    and out her window she did fly,
into the hazy dark alleys of opium
    dens and gaming houses,
unwavering in her pursuit

of potent uncracked ciphers.

Crossing anew the sacred threshold
    of the Supreme House, she ventured
aimlessly, wildly, and utterly care-free
    through the honeycomb vaults,
vestibules and antechambers.

    She wistfully weaved through
a thinning crowd of congregants
    and roamed amok the column forest,
whirling around them like some drunk,
    ecstatic dervish in a state of divine
perspiration until she fell over dazed
    and breathless by an ablution fount.

She gazed into the pool and was startled
    by the queer image of a handsome youth—
as perplexed as she—staring back at her,
    whose comely face bore the same cuts
and bruises as her own. For a time, stranger
    gazed deeply, longingly at stranger, caressing,
        examining, mimicking, matching
            each movement.

She experienced an entirely foreign satisfaction,
    feeling liberated from the fortified confines
of her reality, safely cradled in the protective hands
    of complete obscurity.

'O Merciful, bless and receive Your servant Majd!
    Count him among the folk who unfailingly
        receive You in their hearts—
            who heed Your warnings
            and Your Signs.'

≈≈≈≈≈≈≈≈

As sure as night follows day,
    she found the men of tasting
congregating along the periphery
    of the inner precinct, trading, as always,
in shard after wondrous shard
    of gnosis from beyond
        the cosmic canopy,
    passing 'round and drinking
from the cup of poverty,
    consuming vintage reserved
        for martyrs and saints
            exclusively.

Unable to bear the weight
    of such perplexing concepts,
she made a move to hide
    behind the nearest column
that she may sup on stray Forms
    unnoticed and in peace,
though it made no real difference
    how much or how little discourse
she overheard, she barely
    understood a thing
but felt the epiphanic impact
    of its talismanic qualities.

No matter how expertly they described
    the taste and effects of the celestial wine,
unless she too became a person of tasting,
    she'd know neither flavor nor influence
except the raw drunkenness and mania
        it would induce.

III

When finally came time for the early morning rites,
    she took her chance and threw the dice once more,
sitting directly within the circle of these hoary men.

    At first, they seemed intrigued by the curious child,
and took pity on him on account of his injuries.
    When the master, Bin Jalāl—gatekeeper of mysteries—
greeted the fresh-faced youth, the youth returned
    his salutations sheepishly. When pressed for a name,
        the youth obliged him.

    'And how old are you, Majd?'
The youth responded truthfully that he was fourteen.
    When pressed on what a boy so young was doing
loitering alone in the sanctum at such an hour,
    he responded less truthfully, citing idleness.

When asked to name the house to which he belonged,
    the youth produced his most grandiose deceit thus far,
proclaiming with confidence the name of a house
    renowned—one of exceedingly high pedigree:

'I am of the noble House of Bilqīs,
that ancient clan long predating
the founding of this blessèd city—
the house of Tā'ī, who composed
the hanging odes that adorn the walls
and columns of this Sanctuary.'

The youth had never seen the color
    of a man's face drain so instantly,
nor had he seen eyes that burned
    with such incandescent heat
        and unchecked malice.

Beside himself, the apoplectic Bin Jalāl
    flew in a rage, grabbed the youth
by the throat, lifting him off his feet
    and proceeded to unleash a torrent
of profanities at the boy and his entire
    house of Bilqīs. He then cursed every one
of his relatives, both dead and living—
    branding them enemies of God, of saint
and martyr, saying he'd take pleasure
    in squeezing the life out of at least one son
        of the filthy whorehouse of Bilqīs

when patrolling guards, drawn by the commotion,
    freed the youth from Bin Jalāl's grip and took the man
of tasting, along with his entire cohort of pantheists,
    into custody, who'd be tried that morn
        and beheaded by nightfall.

        IV

Inconsolable, the girl ran through the halls
    until she collapsed beneath a portico.
She clung to the lip of an ablution fount
    and gazed at the queer visage in the pool
staring back at her—a bruised
    and battered figure bearing a fresh red mark
around his throat
        left by the eminent man of tasting
    now condemned to die.

She stared at the image of the youth—
    who wept, and cursed the sky, the stars,
the heavenly orbs, and blasphemed fate
    as she did—until, incensed, she dashed
away the image in a fit, splashing water
    into the face of a woman sitting nearby

who, until then, had paid no mind to anything
  but the brass begging bowl in front of her.

The youth apologized profusely,
but the woman waved away the matter
  and calmly used her sleeves to dry her face.

    'I'm so sorry,
        please forgive me!'

The woman gazed upon the face
  of the bashful youth.
Sukayna, as she introduced herself,
  looked concerned at the wretched state
of this distraught and battered child
wandering the Sanctuary so late at night—
  unaccompanied and vagrant.

Sukayna comforted the comely youth,
  whose eyes had been worn out
by the sheer volume of tears
  that continued to steadily roll
    down his cheeks.

  Sukayna was captivated
and profoundly sympathetic toward him,
  and her maternal instinct compelled her
to comfort the disconsolate boy, urging him
  to confide in her about his state
    and the source of his distress.

Maintaining his masquerade, Majd
  collected himself and took some time
to reply to the woman by weaving
  a narrative that would protect his motives
and identity, but his mind was clouded
  by such intense emotions, and his heart
was so heavy with hopelessness and doubt

that even masquerading passably
    was a bleak prospect.

Sukayna learned of the boy's dire
domestic situation and the inordinate,
    routine violence he had endured;

that what his mother called delinquency
    was in fact an existential rupture,
sparked during the Aḍhā Festival
    while circumambulating the Banyan Tree,
when he caught shards of mystic insight
    from the men of tasting—secrets absent
from every sermon he had ever heard
      from any cleric.

As a near-permanent resident of the Sanctuary
    since renouncing the material world decades ago,
Sukayna was aware of the circle of men
    the youth bemoaned—and of their brand
of metaphysics, which she found overindulgent
      and rife with incongruities.

'Remember that men of tasting know nothing
    if not the essence and virtue of compassion,
for if that does not sustain their bodies,
    what have they to offer a needy soul?

They wish to be discreet, to hold close
    the keys to their treasuries,
when, in reality, they are destitute,
    for only She holds the Sovereign Key
to unlock the gates to the supernal Fount
    of liquid light that is the source
      of all treasuries.

It is by way of compassion that the Real
reveals Herself as the true hidden treasure
    that longs to be recognized.

    The love of the Creator for Her creatures
        is infinite.

To know their Maker, every creature
    must recognize Her in every contour,
crevasse and kernel. Only then
    will they taste the flowing ambrosial waters
        of Her paradisal pleasure gardens.'

In her words, the youth recognized signs
    of the Unseen—of the unknowable realities
of things as they really are,
    which revealed to him the Knowledge
she housed of the Monadic mysteries,
    thereby revealing how advanced she was
        in her own wayfaring—
far more advanced than the hypocrites
    who shunned the youth,
who suddenly seemed like false prophets.

To console Majd, the woman took a dinar
    from her brass bowl, clenched it, whispered
something mysterious into her fist,
    blew into it, then opened her palm—
and lo! to the youth's amazement,
    she unveiled a stunning
        purple lotus blossom.

This theophanic display induced
    a moment of ecstasy that Majd
accepted as a divine portent.
    The youth embraced the mystic
and begged that she accept him

as her devotee.

Sukayna's instinct was to decline
   the boy's request. She felt unfit,
nor did she have the means to be a guide,
   never mind the time to take on a child
      who was in such a fragile state.

More concerning yet, she was aware
   of the potential repercussions
of her refusing the child, and decided
   in the moment simply to recite the Names
and Formulæ, confident that it would,
   at minimum, ameliorate the boy's current
      physical and existential malaise.

≈≈≈≈≈≈≈≈

For several days the boy never left her side,
   and Sukayna eventually accepted the reality
that he simply had no home to return to—
   at least not voluntarily.

If he did, how much worse must it be
   than being a homeless child?

In her heart, she ceded all understanding
   to the Knowing, the Accepter of the needy,
the abandoned and the destitute.
   Truly all knowledge and magnanimity
      belong to Her.

V

From the very first, she was astonished
by the boy's ability to mimic her recitations
   with maximal precision

and minimal flaw.

She immediately recognized how rare
    a treasure he was and took his receptivity
and capacity as signs, while accepting
    the ever-increasing burden the All-Merciful
        had placed on her.

Soon Sukayna became so deeply attached to the boy
    that she felt compelled to venture into subtler matters
and to impart knowledge exclusively revealed to her
    by the Real through whom creation ever blooms.

The youth's unwavering determination
    to advance beyond the great divide and into the sea
of the *mysterium fascinosum* was ferocious,
    and she would do everything in her power
    to aid his passage.

Having spent several days reciting with pure intent
    the Names, the Formulæ, and verses of scripture,
    Sukayna bade the boy follow her.
The two of them circumambulated the Banyan,
    day and night, well into the early hours of morn.

    When they retired, instead of sleeping,
they silently meditated upon the Merciful,
    who mercifully kept their brass bowl
        filled with alms.

They moved almsgivers to such a degree
    that the givers themselves felt compelled
to contemplate the Divine with more concerted
        effort and earnestness.

After a week of circumambulating the Great Banyan,
    Sukayna began revealing to Majd everything she knew
about the subtle meanings of the Names and Letters.

She revealed the holy mysteries of the rising lights,
of the most guarded treasures hidden in the depths
    of eternity without beginning, and eternity without end,

of accidents that bloom from both desire and defect,
    of the unnamed named and the unqualified qualifier,
of the non-existent existent and its precise inverse,
    of the holy saying, 'Whoever finds Me never loses Me.'

She spoke of the insentient beings that glorify the Real
with 'Yea, O Lord of Mercy, yea indeed, O Most Beneficent,'
    and the human heart that responds in perfect kind,

of the hand serving as the shore of its own ocean
    that hails lost ships to port at the turning of the tide,

of those who stepped on that dry land carrying boon
    that turned to stone the very moment they set foot,

of the rising Throne and the setting of the Footstool,
    of the covenant between Creator and Her creation,

    of the utterly imminent and entirely transcendent
nature of the One who Testifies against all souls,
    whose adjudications ranks of angels shall uphold,

of the commingling of jinn and human natures,
    of wavering between, then breaking the two desires,

of unveiling and navigating the realms within realms,
    of the Hidden, the Manifest, and the third eye,

of 'Let the seventy-thousand mysteries of My Majesty
    pass through the heart of the gnostic and cause them
to turn and overturn in the night,' and 'You are My Names
    and the proof of My Essence. My Quality is yours
        and yours is Mine.

You are My throne, My mirror,
    My dwelling place, My hidden treasure,
My locus of Self-disclosure.
    So which of My Signs do you deny?'

With each passing hour, the dust of the mundane
    steadily cleared, and the boy's path increasingly
came into focus, though it remained strewn
    with obstacles,
                            and the threat of ambush
by ego's ravenous, marauding riders
        was ever-present.

The youth knew nothing of the imaginal isthmus.
    How would he know how to navigate its shores,
let alone engage with the subtle entities therein
    without the lamp of a guide to lead him
out of the darkness and into the clearing light?
        And so, Sukayna guided him.

Through meditation, the youth slipped
    into a state of sukūn
for the very first time,
    and Sukayna's spirit-conscience met his,
and hand in hand they flew
    from their material bodies
and landed on the isthmian shores,
    where he sat with his master
and observed the *barzakh's* strange mystique—
    not least the fact that
wherever the youth placed his hands,
    it glowed with a curious
        blue candescence
            that dimmed away
    the moment he lifted them.

In the unlit realm of the in-between,
the melodious sound of Sukayna's voice
    reciting the divine Names and Letters
by some strange alchemy revived his spirit.
    Sukayna continued to instruct him
in the science of the Letters and Names.
    Incredibly, in the isthmian realm,
the youth could not only mentally perceive,
    but see, touch, feel, eat, and drink them,
and they nourished both his subtle
    spirit-conscience and his material body.

She traced ciphers in the sand that glowed,
    revealing nuances that induced successive
epiphanic states that propelled him
    to transcend his own spirit-conscience
        and enter the pleroma.

Had Sukayna not described them so masterfully,
he would have been barred from the essence
    of their metacosmic qualities.

She introduced him to the seven recitation methods
    of the Cylopiad from the seven regions of the Zāgra.
She trained him in the correct pronunciation
    of every part of every letter of every word
of the first section of Her infallible scripture
    before advancing to the stage of memorization—
this was due to the sheer complexity of the script
    which cannot be self-taught solely from the Book,
        but must be transmitted by a master
            from their master
    linked along the chain of transmission
all the way back to the messenger Barā᾿
    the epochal prophet and tongue of the Unseen
who received the Cylopiad himself

from the angel Elia in the age of ignorance.

Sukayna trained him to be proficient,
to give each Letter its due, and to obsess
        over its articulation.
    This ensured that the text is recited
  precisely the way it was revealed
        to the Prophet Barāʾ.

She taught him the seventeen
    articulation points in the vocal tract
where the Letters are produced
    and how they interact
when they meet and mingle.

He learned how each Letter
    has eternal and conditional qualities
that amplify its traces in the dome
    of the dark empyrean
        and upon the two horizons.

This practice of journeying to the isthmus
and tutoring the youth in the ways of the Real
    went on for weeks, and by season's turning,
in the days leading up to the Aḍḥā Festival
    of Sacrificial Slaughter, worshippers passing
through the north-eastern portico of the holy
    precinct were enthralled by their recitations.

    They filled the portico with music
of the spheres, seducing many
        to sit and listen for hours on end.

On the morning of the Aḍḥā Festival,
the alms flowed like manna
    from the generous hands of the Bounteous.

Pilgrims filled the honeycomb halls,
sat opposite one another in row
    upon endless row and broke their fast
with dates and ambrosial water
    just as the call for midday rites
        rang all throughout the Sanctuary.

All through the day, swathes of pilgrims
    performed their circumambulations
and exchanged salutations,
        invoking the Names
    of the Beneficent Master
and engaging in supererogatory
        acts of generosity.

In the bustling agoras, lambs were slaughtered,
slow-roasted and served with saffron yoghurt,
    honey, fig and flax bread to the poor
        and the orphaned.

The city's taverns and gaming houses
were allowed to open their doors to patrons
    as early or as late as they pleased
        without censure.

The zephyr of glad tidings passed through the porticos
and honeycomb-vaulted halls of the Grand Sanctuary.
    Yet unbeknownst to Majd—whose locks had grown long
and whose tunic had become worn from constant exposure
    to the elements—the youth was spotted by a relative
on this most joyous day of celebration and sacrifice,
    and by night the news had reached his household.

≈≈≈≈≈≈≈≈

When dawn spread out her orient beams
over the two horizons, Sukayna and Majd
    had already performed their ablution rites
and circumambulations around the Banyan.
    They spent the day in a state of serene sukūn
tracing signs and ciphers in isthmian sands
    and memorizing verses of the Cylopiad.

And at sunset, when they retired to their portico,
    after they broke bread, drank honeyed milk
and ate their dates over cups of jasmine tea,
    the old master unclasped the amulet she wore
around her neck and gave it to the youth,
    who she had grown so fond of—a token
in the tradition of gift-giving on the first day
    of the week-long Aḍhā Festival of Sacrifice.

Inscribed on it in marvelous calligraphy
        were the words:

'Merciful, Living, Light
    of the Heavens and Earth.'

Majd received it graciously,
    overcome with emotion.

He ran his fingers over the precious amulet.
    An unusual energy radiated from this rare artifact,
the talismanic effect of which filled the boy's being
    with the light of compassion that so characterized
        his new master and spiritual guardian.

The youth clasped it around his neck and clutched it,
    vowing to himself to wear it as long as he lived.

Sukayna conveyed to him the esoteric
    and exoteric meanings of the inscription,
tracing each word back to its etymological root,
    expounding and unveiling the gnosis

that lay beyond each letter's curvature,
        and every diacritic
    that dictated its pronunciation.

At the end of every lesson,
    she would guide him
into a state of sukūn—they'd meet
    on the shores of the isthmus
and, as spirit-consciences,
    freely roam its vistas.

There, the master introduced the boy
    to a host of martyrs and messengers—
from vicegerents of the Real, to sages
        once blinded
    who'd regained their sight
and were given salvific visions—
    the kind reserved for those whose hearts
are well-prepared to receive them—
    to heroines and heroes of late epic
        Traxionic poetry
    who the youth assumed
        were purely mythical.

More than anything, at this point
    along his isthmian journeying,
meeting the literary figures
    that he dearly cherished—whose names
and deeds and conceits and conflicts
    and devastating mutual destruction
are permanent imprints in his imagination—
    surprised and deeply satisfied.

He marveled at how these once-fabled beings
    made manifest in his imagination
glided across the isthmian waters
    on horseless chariots,

> disembarking on the shores
>> to greet the old master
>>> and her gifted apprentice

when the youth was violently jerked
> from his state of meditation by a voice
that shrieked his name, his given name,
> the one she had deliberately obscured.

> The startled girl had not the chance to register
the identity of the assailant who seized her
> by her locks and struck her across the face.

Zulaykẖa exposed her daughter's disguise
> before a stupefied Sukayna, who was then
ambushed by marshals who unleashed
> an onslaught of violence upon the woman.

Āyā yelled and flailed in vain as the battered
> Sukayna was torn away from her.
The mother grabbed her pitiful, vagrant girl
> and dragged her by her locks through the streets
of Heliopolis, publicly humiliating her only child
> on this most holy day of the Sacrificial Slaughter.

Charges of defilement and corruption of youth
> were leveled against Sukayna and upheld
>> by a jury of magistrates.

On the morning of the second day
> of the Aḍḥā Festival, Sukayna
was beheaded in the central agora,
> along with twenty-seven luckless
women accused of sorcery —
> the news of which the mother
took great pleasure in delivering
> as she beat her daughter to exhaustion.

Sensoria

I hear You. From the East to the West
the zephyr blows traces of You,
and in them I sense You.

    But like the zephyr,
those traces quickly disappear
    and I'm left believing the absurdity
that we are apart.

And when the zephyr passes,
    it is replaced with whispers of doubt
that I had heard any trace of You at all.

I hear You. From North to South,
I hear Your Name named by every tongue
and lauded by every creed. Ambrosial Names!
No matter what form You take, I recognize You.

And when the zephyr scatters You,
    I want to kill myself,
then I remember that Zephyr
    is a name that also belongs to You.

A Name that scatters traces of Names!
I hear them and lack all understanding.

I hear You manifesting unrelentingly,
in the groans of Gāiā as she eats and births
Herself, in the sprouting roots of the living,
in the rot and decay of the dying,
in the laments and exaltations of songbirds,
in the trembling leaves,

in the snapping branches,
    in the sound of fruit falling
        and the consequent thump
            as they hit the ground.

I lack all understanding
    and hear You all the same.

I hear You rhymed and unrhymed
    without reason.

No matter the arrangement of Your syllables,
no matter how corrupted or masterful
    the recitation of You,
no matter how contorted
    or distorted the pronunciation,
no matter how subtle
    or gross the insight,
no matter how soft or abrasive
    the tone or timbre.

You are the subject and object of all recitations,
    and in that my belief is unwavering.

Indeed, You are manifest in these
    and infinitely more ways,
and I am grateful,
    but *why* do I hear You?

≈≈≈≈≈≈≈≈

I see You. On every page, I find You there.
When I read You, I laugh
    because I keep finding You.
You mock me when I turn the page
    and You're not there,
then mock me when I cry
    and wet the page,

and when the salty-ink admixture
    runs down and stains my skin,
I am completely humiliated by You.

In despair, I rip You out and toss You.
Then to atone for my violent act,
    I turn inward,
and in the confines of my being,
        there You are! Laughing.

I see You. In the dark,
    You are absence and substance,
and so, You frighten me.
    In the light, You are the sun,
and so, You burn me.
    When I take shelter from You
in the shade, You expose me!
    I look down and realize
I am naked, and for that You mock me,
    and I am humiliated.

I shiver naked in Your shadow, curse the cold,
then shamelessly return to You for warmth
and the right to bathe in You. How shameful!
    How humiliating.

I see You in the straightness of form,
I see You in the form of straightness.
I see You in the curvature of form,
I see You in the form of curvature.

In asymptotes I see but cannot meet You.
Parabolæ begin and terminate in You.

As proof, You are abstract. As abstract,
        You are proof.

There You are, occurring and recurring
    naturally and unnaturally.
In denotation and connotation, You again!

Numerable and innumerable, phenomenal
and supernal. Verity and error bend
        at Your behest.

How absurd!
    The more I learn,
        the less I know of You,

and so, I remain perpetually ignorant
        but ever aware of You.

I see You there, scattered across the hemisphere.
How splendid is Your panoply of bodies,
moons, and mansions! The Northern Lights
        envy You,

    Vernal Dictator, Autumnal Keeper!
Celestial whirlpool, vega, nebula, dysnomia,
    You, You, You! You lunar, You solar,
Queen Andromeda, King Oberon,
    Alpha Centauri, You the rising,
You the setting—look at You combusting
        and burning out unthinkingly.

I see Cosmic You inhaling and exhaling You!
    How sublime You are, flanked
by Your esteemed retinue.
    How does an ignorant sycophant
        fit in Your design?

Indeed, I see You manifest in all these ways,
present and immediate, wherever I set my sights,
and I am grateful, but *why* do I see You?

A. A. Telmesani

≈≈≈≈≈≈≈≈

On my fingertips, I feel You.
 I bury my hands in You,
I can feel You in my fingernails.
 And when I shake You off, I scatter You.
In the meadows, groves, and pastures,
 I walk barefoot, that I may feel
Your tufts between my toes.
 By the stream, in the soft clay,
I press my hands into You,
 and when I lift them, there You are!
The cuneiform code of You.
 Had You not stripped me
of my discerning faculties,
 I would decipher You.

In the North, I feel You.
 On Cerulean shores,
You invite me in,
 and so I wade into You,
ice-cold and up to my knees in You.
I feel You trying to drag me under,
  but I resist.

Then You roll, rise and crash over me.
Down I go, like a stone submerged in You.
I feel You filling my lungs and sense the fear
of drowning in You, until You spit me out
and leave me gasping for You! Every time
 I resist, You drag down.
But when I give in, You return me to shore,
floating in You.

 In the South, I feel You.
  The earthy breaths

of the pistachio trees fill my lungs
as I walk through You.
    In the foliage,
there You are! Crunching
    beneath my feet.
Along my path, I find You
    every now and then
uprooted, fallen, rotting,
    obstructing my path.
And when I place my hand
    and hop over You,
spores fly and I get splinters
    of You in my skin.

One by one, I pull You out.
    How difficult You are
sometimes! When I get lost in You
    after dark, or I am caught in the rain,
I find a hollow and shelter in You.
    How long will I remain in You?

From East to West, from the floodplains
to the steppes, from Hazar to Anbūrām,
I roam You. And when I am weary,
I drag my feet in You, surveying You.
I feel every pebble in my pathway.
And when You sink below the horizon,
I set up camp and wait for You to rise again.
As You rise and fall, I yearn to behold
Your orient rays and bathe in You.

The more I feel of You, the less I understand.
    How much more is there of You?

On my fingertips, across my skin,
through my hair, beneath my feet,
and in my lungs, there's no avoiding

the feel of You, but *why* do I feel You?
Undoubtedly, I am the lord of ignorance
    and You are Knowing.

So make me understand!
    If I keep hearing You,
and I keep seeing You,
    and I keep feeling You,
wheresoever I go, then why
    do I still have doubts about You?
Is it form or is it substance
    that deludes me
        and obscures You?

Will I ever perceive
    Your Self-disclosure?
What part of me must be pried open
    in order to find You?
Why do I love wayfarers
    but not the Guide?
Why do I trust the servant
    but not the Master—
        the subject
    but not the Object?

Why are the writings of saints
    more sacred to me than You?
Why do I love so fiercely the idea
    of loving You, but find it impossible
to just love You without
    qualification or impediment?
Why are there strings attached?

If I hear and see and feel You all the time,
    but spend my days doubting sensoria
summarily, are You just a foreign entity
    possessing and tormenting me?

I just want to understand.
     Loose me from myself!
I am impatient, defective,
     and afraid of my own naivety.

I suppose, if ignorance is my slavedriver,
          there is no other recourse but to till the field,
sow You, tend to You, harvest and deliver You,
          then watch as others consume You
               at my expense.

I will till the field, sow and harvest.
     But when the time is right,
I will raise Gāiā from the very Earth.
     I will be one of the dirt-eaters
who stuff themselves with You.
     I will ambush the overseer
and spring myself from bondage.
     I will haunt the Zāgra Valley as a fugitive.
I will scour the floodplains.
     I will feed on the mud and clay.
I will chart the course of nothing.
     I will mark the days on my wrists
          and lose c o u n t.

And when I've soaked the Earth,
  and there's nothing left of me,
     I will give to Gāiā
          and await my verdict.

≈≈≈≈≈≈≈≈

Like the zephyr, traces disappear.
Give my regards to the overseer.
Say to them, 'It had to be this way.'

Return to Ḥarak

I

And Yāsīn tended the grove
   in the day, in the delicate
sunlight dancing between
   the leaves of sprawling crowns,
moving by the gentle hand
   of the Unmoved Mover.

Most nights he retired
   in the generous shadow
of a low-hanging fig tree,
   as was his preference,
and at dawn, we watched him
   perform his ablutions
with water from the vessel
   we had placed beside him
before he fell asleep
   under whichever tree
     he chose for shelter.

All the while we burned with questions
   we knew he had answers to,
and yet we refrained from asking.

Upon our arrival from Heliopolis,
   he retreated from our imploring eyes
to the hermitage across the ford
   upstream from the monastery,
where he remained with Leāna

for forty days, and for forty days
    we did not see him.

And when he returned to us one morning
    on the forty first day of his sojourn,
he returned a being revived, but ever so,
    for the injured look did not escape him.

Throughout his eighteen-month tenure
    as caretaker of the monastery,
we refrained from probing him,
    despite our incurable curiosity
and queries regarding his forty-day
    retreat in the hermitage up the hill—
and the wisdom imparted by Leāna
    regarding Self-disclosures unveiled
by the Hidden, the Manifest,
        exclusively to her
concerning the cosmic hierarchies,
    the stations and waystations
of the rising lights,
    celestial orbs and bodies,
        their mysteries
and the keys to their treasuries.

How difficult it was
    withholding our barrage!

But we were marred by guilt, and perhaps
    a sense of obligation to allow him to heal.
But inside, I felt the burden of guilt tenfold,
    for it was because of me that Yāsīn suffered so.

Was it not I who was thrown
    into the lion's den
before the multitudes of Heliopolis
    at the Colossei Gladitorium?

I would gladly be torn apart by the lions,
resurrected and torn apart all over again
     if it would mend a fraction of him.
But in his mind, he alone bore the guilt.
     He wished he had never divulged
a single shard of gnosis to Huthayfa
     within earshot of anyone—let alone publicly,
in the heart of the Holy House
     in the month of Dhul Qiʿdah,
where his words first caught our ears.

We say there are records left behind
     and yet to come that will testify
on our behalf, when our own
     transgressions shall testify against us,
when She who takes account of all
     shall fulfill Her cosmic designs,
when Creation at long last
          swallows herself.

When we departed in the evening
     from the sanctum of the Banyan Tree
where we congregated every day,
     and returned to him by morning
black and blue with broken bones
     from nightly beatings, he relied
on his Vast Earth alchemy
     to mend our bodies—but our spirits
could not be crushed by kindred hands,
     for we had so willingly given ourselves
          to him.

Ultimately, it was our own guilt
     against Yāsīn's—
guilt upon guilt,
     and a lifetime of psycho-

emotional scarring.

So, for nearly two years, we did as he did,
   lived as he lived, ate what he ate, tended
what he tended, practiced, prayed,
   kept morning, noon, and evening vigil
in the crypt, in the grove, on the clay
   by the ford of the stream just as he did —
      nothing more nor less.

Following his way of living
   was like following the soul's natural arc,
guided by the same compassionate force
   that moves the celestial bodies along
their precise precalculated courses —
   Her engendering Command
      made manifest.

   II

When the caretaker forced her way
   out of retirement and banished Yāsīn
to the fig grove, it was a great boon to us.

   Our sage instruction was the silent study
of the motions of his body, the care with which
   he handled every stem, leaf, fig and vine.

We heard him recite the sacred Names
   and Formulæ and we recited them verbatim
to ourselves, committing them to memory,
   etching them into the very kernels of our being,
whether or not we understood the contents
   of their abundant storehouses of gnosis.

In the meantime, we slipped slowly
into the familiar trades from our past lives

prior to conversion.

This was true for my dear friends,
    but not for me. I had neither trade
nor craft—neither skill inherent
    nor proclivity toward anything
worthy or of any use to anyone,
    but my strings were easy to pluck
and my attention over-indulgent
    and fueled by youthful energy.

           III

I came to know King Huthayfa
    in the labyrinthine aisles
of the stone library archives,
    where I harassed him for verse
and lore of the Zāgra—of her clans
    and monarchies, and insisted
on hearing the chains of transmission
    to verify each tale's authenticity.

    How ignorant I was
       of kin and country!

What glorious epochs and lineages
    of prophets, sages, and messengers!

What marvelous beings of wisdom
    who stoke Imagination's raging fires!

On one occasion, he showed me
    a marvelous map—the first I had ever seen—
of the Zāgra Valley and her territories
    and her source of life, the River Zāgra.

    I pointed to the city of Tā Nūn
and asked Huthayfa—servant of the Real

and Her vicegerent Yāsīn son of Roā,
saying, 'O king, who are the esteemed poets
    renowned among the tribes of Tā Nūn?'

And Huthayfa replied, 'Āyā, dear,
    long is the line of laureates of Tā Nūn—
jewel of southern Dārsabaʿīn.
    Can you not name a single one?'

    I bowed and shook
        my head in shame.

Out of pity, he listed the names of men
    and the names of their daughters
and sons, their houses and the jinn
    muses associated with their most
esteemed poets. He recounted the names
    and dates of wars between the houses
of Tuffāj and Shādūr and Turūkān,
    their outcomes, resulting marriage
alliances, and the names of their progeny—
    all of which he recited from memory.

Then I pointed to Heliopolis and asked,
    'O king, who are the esteemed poets
of my people and the jinn muses
    associated with their verse-craft?'

    Pitying the extent of my ignorance,
Huthayfa, with eyes glinting, waxed
    lyrical of Tāʾī of the house of Bilqīs,
that ancient clan of the Founded City,
    reciting one of his many hanging odes.

'And it is said,' Huthayfa continued
    'that Ashtūrumāzda, Queen of jinn,
placed her yoke upon the tongue
    of Tāʾī of the house of Bilqīs

on his third birthday, the moment
    he first recited from the Cylopiad.'

O to have a jinnī queen as a muse!
    I thought to myself.

And he continued, 'What about Sihām,
    daughter of Yaqzān of the House of Kāf
whose qaṣā'id and quatrains command
    the pages of anthologies in libraries
of wealthy city-states from Gālibūr to Qays,
    and whose zajal and muwashshaḥāt
can be heard along the silk roads
    in the ancient ballads of the bedouin?'

    I shook my head
        in complete ignorance.

     'I've heard directly,'
    the ex-regent continued,
'from the mouths of estimable poets
    from honored tribes all throughout
the central valley who spread poison
    out of envy, who rashly mock
Sihām the daughter of Yaqzān.
    They accuse her of being yoked
by a *nasnās*—spawn of a woman raped
    by the *shiqq* demon Rā, who roams
        the lowlands along the East River.

But they only poison themselves.
    Their lame verse will be swept
from history by the eternal spring
    of Sihām's bounteous dawāwīn.

Her jinn muse is widely known
    by human and subtle beings alike
to be Azāzūl of the line of Vashram,

who fell from the station of *jīm*
to the place where the Zāgra splits,
    where he possessed a mute youngling—
Yaḥyā of the house of Kāf—
    and returned with/in him
        to the Founded City.

The first words that Yaḥyā's kin
    heard him speak in his life
were not his own, but Azāzūl's,
    who produced from the boy
what would become the first
    of some ten thousand qaṣā'id
which would adorn the vast halls
    of the Sanctuary at Heliopolis.

Azāzūl—who yoked the tongues
    of Thurāyā and Yasmīn and Rā'id
and the rest of the long line of fine
    poets of Kāf, all of whom shrink
in the shadow of the saint of Yaqzān,
    the supreme poet of her honored clan.'

And King Huthayfa carried on,
    listing five more Heliopolite poets,
their honored houses and the names
    and lineages of their jinn muses

before I slipped away unnoticed
    as he struggled to recall a couplet.

        IV

On other sojourns to the archives,
I marveled at the deeply devoted Ḥakkān
of the Ṣamaḍī clan—
    that noble house
and rightful guardian of that hallowed place,

that sanctum where the sacred Banyan
blooms everlasting in the very heart
of the Zāgra Valley—
        whose line
has borne the burden of custodianship
for well over five hundred years.

Many houses—honored and disgraced—
have for centuries incurred the wrath
of many tribes in the central valley,
especially of other Heliopolite factions.

Blood feuds stain all clans and houses
except one—the house of Ṣamaḍī,
whose burden demanded deference
from everyone.
        Theirs is a house
unblemished, nigh as sacred as
the hallowed ground that is their keep.

Truly, Ḥakkān son of Layla Ṣamaḍī,
        nephew of his eminence, Raḍwān
the custodian of the sanctum sanctorum,
        sole caretaker of the Great Banyan—
that bezel of the all-bounteous Creator,
        that locus of manifestation in the world
of bodies, that unique entry point
        of imaginal entities and corporeous
                bodies of subtle nature.

He was favored by the Beginningless
        Benefactress with boundless knowledge
of the twenty-eight stations of the Letters
        unleashed by Aleph in the Great Becoming—
those mansions that housed the mysteries
        of all that was, all that is, and all that will be.

This unique gnosis was evident
    in his love of the science of Letters
and Names both divine and profane,
    of philology and grammatical artifacts
that carry news of borrowed words
    brought in by the zephyr
on the foreign tongues of poets
    and caravan merchants;
in the code of the vandal, in the ciphers
    of the mendicant, and in the tractates
of sage philosophers who yearn
    and roam the Zāgra endlessly.

The son of Layla Ṣamaḍī excelled
    in his understanding of the subtleties
of dialectal variants, of polyglossic
    registers and their bastardizations.
He mastered the refined and vulgate
    tongues of every region and tribe,
for the mysteries of the Letters
    and Names allowed him to decode
        the conceits of Language itself.

The house of Ṣamaḍī is granted
    an exalted place in the Sanctuary,
where Ḥakkān spent his days and nights
    reading the hanging odes and verses
of the poets of Kāf and Bilqīs
    and Sufrāzūrī and Ḥākimī.

He's since traded that sacred shrine
    for Ḥarak's archives and its treasuries
that teem with sage canonical wisdom,
    where he pored over scrolls and codices
brimming with mellifluent odes from ancient
    dawāwīn from the most exotic lands.

I picked up a habit of surprising him,
    pointing randomly at a strange script
and asking, 'What language is that?'
    and he would say something like,
'That is Early Kūfic, the tongue
    of your ancestors in the dialect
        of ʿAqqād in the East Delta.'

One time, I pointed to lines
    of poetry in a script so alien,
I assumed it was literal code,
    but then he said, 'that is Wardī,
one of the major native dialects
    spoken in the mountainous regions
of Southern Anbūr, and a vulgate
    tongue of the Ḥarbite tribes.'

I asked him to recite this poetry,
    and as he did, the words flowed as if
from the very source of the Real's
    eternal fount, like manna soaked
in amber honey that ran sweetly
    into my ears, animating the inanimate
        crevices of my pitiful being.

Overwhelmed, I left the library
    that night weeping in a mess,
struck by the devastating beauty
    of a language I did not understand.

V

Some nights, I would return
    to the archives and find Layth
Kutbī of the Heliopolite Kutbiyyā—
    that house of master bookbinders

and papyri pressers who provide
    their services to the ascetic poet
and the civic administrator alike,
    whose hired hands have also bound
the rarest of Zāgran manuscripts
    kept in the catacomb archives
of the Great Library at Heliopolis.

How fortunate were we, then, to have
    a son of Kutbī tending to the withered
        spines and crumbling papyri
    of invaluable scrolls and codices
        available to us there
            in the Ḥarak archives?

Are they not the receptacles and couriers
    that tell the tale of our civilization?

I asked if I could watch him mend
    and bind, that I might assist him.
Though flattered, Layth preferred
    to work on his own. He did allow me
to watch him craft, so I learned silently.

    Those skills have sadly dissipated
from memory, but watching Layth
    work silently as he bound and repaired
taught me the subtleties of craft
    and the devotion required for mastery.

A natural consequence of his vocation
    was gaining an insatiable love
        for Knowledge.

I have yet to meet a less discriminating
    reader of literature.
Not one work—
however licit or illicit it was

to the legal dogmatists—
was off-limits.

Layth entirely lacked the existential fear
    that they had of accidentally
"converting to the faiths of infidels"
    simply from reading their scriptures
and considering points of view
        that challenged theirs.

    This fear, in fact, proved
        that they were weak,
            and that their faith
            and convictions
                were fragile.

His intimate knowledge of the schools
    of philosophy, the natural sciences
and the great dawāwīn of Kūfic poets
        from across the Zāgra
            remains nothing short
                of extraordinary.

He waxed of his love of poetry
    like a true craftsman, enough
to deceive the shrewdest skeptic
    of his aversion to *writing* verse.

His thoughts were cumbersome
    and weighty with wisdom and logic
that suited the philosophic allegory—
    a fountain he would drink from
        for the rest of his days.

VI

Returning from Durusān one day,
    I discovered along the stone path
that led to the sacred fig grove
    a stunning scene from an ancient
Heliopic myth chiseled in relief
    by some divinely guided hand
        gifted with hereditary knowledge.

I ran my fingers over the relief,
    following the carving's curvatures
from right to left, up and down.
    My ignorant interpretation
was of a half human, half lion
    demigod leading an army
of Turkānids on elephants
    and gallant steeds, flanked
by herds of strange four-footed
    creatures I did not recognize.
The detail, hewn in solid granite
    was beyond all comprehension.

It could only be the work of Kāi
    son of Taīna, pride
        of the house of Jāfarī.

    He spent much of his time hunched
over some new section of the path,
    legs crossed with chisel and stone,
engraving with imperceptible motion
    while seemingly holding his breath.

As curious as I was insufferable,
    I'd ask Kāi often if I could sit
and watch him cut stone silently
    and he'd always acquiesce

for reasons of great mystery to me
   with a subtle nod and a smile.
To my unfair benefit he seemed
   unbothered or undisturbed
by my inane and idle voyeurism.

   I was always tempted to ask him
what scene and from which myth
   he was currently depicting,
but I refrained from requesting
   detailed ekphrasis until evening
when we would tend the fig grove
   alongside Yāsīn and the others.

But Kāi was no mythologist,
   or specialist in Heliopic lore.

The convoluted extrapolations
   of folk traditions and sacred history
that Kāi enthusiastically described
   were masterpieces of elliptical,
philosophic abstract narratives
   that bordered on the acrobatic.

And so, I relied on our self-abdicated King
   Huthayfa's vast treasuries of knowledge
to recount every myth in its entirety—
   the source-text, the names and dates
of battles, warriors, mythic creatures,
   gods, demigods, beings of light
and smokeless fire and the specific
   Cylopiadic verses that some scenes
      were evidently adaptations of.

VII

Every week brought at least a pair
   of new reliefs, each one a unique
work of unfathomable artisanry
   that told the story of our ancestry.

The ebbing and flowing imagery
   of mortal and immortal beings,
of subtle and substantial elements,
   was the stuff of the imaginal realm—
that world of suspended and fleeting
   images where the worlds of spirits
and bodies commingle—or of Gāiā's
   Vast Earth, where the Calamus
marked Her final resting place.

   In these sublimely cut depictions
of Heliopic scenes, I came to know,
   or perhaps was marginally able to
demystify the mysterious matrix
   of Kāi the stonecutter's wild mind.

One day, I spotted Kāi and a group
   of younger monks erecting scaffolding
around the southern monastery entrance.
   Surely, I thought, the caretaker
would never sanction such a project—
   one she'd dismiss automatically
as an overindulgent display
   of calligraphic stonemasonry.

Yet there she was, transporting planks
   twice her size to Kāi and his assistants.

I went to Cāto the Elder to inquire
   and was astounded to hear that he too,

along with Leāna, acquiesced to Kāi's
    request to adorn the entryways
of the monastery with calligraphic
    renderings of the Names and Formulæ.

Even they were susceptible to Kāi's spell—
    both easily seduced and slain by his sorcery.
And of course, the artisanry evident
    in the relief-work was simply exceptional.

Those who now enter the free-standing gate
    recognize the sanctity of those hallowed grounds
by the Names and Formulæ that rain on them
    like manna as they enter that sacred precinct.

    VIII

By the ford of the stream, in the soft clay,
    with her calamus in hand and a look
of incomparable determination,
    I would find Māyā fervidly tracing
tessellations in a variety of permutations
        all along the windy bank.

All day, Māyā worked on innovative ways
    of replicating the cosmic code *ad infinitum*
in its unique perfection among the genera
    of Forms, prime matter and Vast Earth mud,
and in the night, when the sun robbed her
    of light to work with, she collected water,
wet the clay along the bank and erased
    by hand every tessellation she painstakingly
produced over the course of that day,
    returning the following morning
        well-prepared to start again,
            only with renewed

determination.

This was the private life
of Māyā the Heliopolite
at the Ḥarak monastery
during our sojourn there.

≈≈≈≈≈≈≈≈

One day, I asked her,
    'What shape is that?'
when the floodgates burst
    and the reservoirs
emptied themselves
    and overwhelmed me.

Māyā described a radical tessellation
achieved by harnessing the square root
    of squares and rectangles unceasingly.

She then launched into the history
    of the discipline and the great masters
who laid down the firm principia
    without which these shapes would be
the sole property of the Vast Earth
    well beyond our own
        imaginal scope.

She revealed that every shape
    that will ever exist already exists
in a place that only the inner eye
    of a soul worn by wayfaring may enter.

Those who enter can convey those Forms
    from the Vast Earth into our world
        of manifest orbs and bodies.

A. A. Telmesani

What extraordinary shapes would Māyā
    traffic if she ever accessed that realm?

Māyā described at length the lineage
    of the great schools of antiquity
starting with the Masriyyūn
    and the Academy at Byblos,
and the school of Amhotep
    the patriarch, builder of empires,
to the Heratic schools at Yūnān
    and their founding matriarch
Shamsiyya Rāz the Ḥabashite
    whose precise calculations
made possible the construction
    of the aqueducts that nourish
the lands and all their inhabitants
    from Dārsaba ʿīn to Gālibūr,
who built the architectural wonders
    of Heliopolis—the Founded City—
and whose thirty-two axioms—
    now codified for all time—
led to the establishment
    of the four schools of Zāgran
        theoretical geometry.

Māyā described the world of Qays,
    who taught at the Library of Buyūtāt
during the reign of Rex Bāshistūr IV,
    where he established the doctrines
of utmost importance in the sciences
    of geometry, astronomy, and astrology
that unveiled new ways of interpreting
    the manifest realities of Self-disclosure.

≈≈≈≈≈≈≈≈

Since the age of ignorance,
    prior to the founding
of the city of Heliopolis,
    problems with the precise
construction of the cubed altar
    and its doubling, with trisecting
the twelve rising asterisms,
    and with the elusive squaring of the circle
had confounded the minds of geometers
    up until the establishment
of Qays' sound alchemical doctrines
    and axioms that were like Vast Earth
contraband hoarded and trafficked
        in quantity.

The supreme geometer at Buyūtāt
    dismantled the twelve postulates
of Faythāghurz—that ancient
    desert patriarch of Gālibūr—
as a beardless adolescent
    under the tutelage of the eminent
Umm Kharja, who produced
    translations of the postulates
in her youth from Tetwānī
    to Middle Kingdom Kūfic.

Māyā described Qays' conic theorems
    then traced out whole diagrams
she had memorized as a young girl.
    She revealed the various possible ways
a cone may intersect a spatial plane
    and how parabolæ and hyperbolæ
helped Qays and the Masriyyūn
    measure the sun's diurnal course.

Manakhmus and Arcimādus of Yūnān,
    whom Māyā extolled with verve,

were said to have geometrized
    the manifest cosmic hierarchies
and revealed the courses of solar
    and lunar bodies and their epicycles.

They also transcribed musical modes
    from the twelve fixed constellations
revealing the natural harmonic degrees
    and intervallic relationships that yield
            the astral music
                of the spheres.

For Māyā, however, her infatuation
    with these epochal master geometers
was focused on their original
    innovations and inventions of radical
tessellations based on perfect ratios
    that could not have existed anywhere
other than the realm of the Real
    through whom creation blooms.

Māyā took to tracing these tessellations
    with her calamus in the soft wet clay,
all day, every day without taking sabbath,
    and the bank of the stream would teem
with variations of shapes that were somehow
    wrought by these impossibly perfect ratios.

I swear that I saw creatures passing by
    who stumbled onto these diagrams
and stared at them intently, as if literate
    in that coded language,
        then scampered away,
    avoiding them with unusual care.

They seemed to recognize the gnostic quality
    of the Master Geometer's sacred code.

And the birds were entertained,
    perched up on their hanging boughs,
and from their superior vantages
    surveyed Māyā's marvelous work.

They transcribed the signs to song
with a preternatural fluency beyond
the fathoming of the human mind.

≈≈≈≈≈≈≈≈

The dominant romantic notion
    that only men of tasting had
the spiritual and intellectual
    capacity to access and convey
such alchemical Formulæ firsthand
    for the benefit of humanity
        had fueled in her
    an all-conquering drive
        to access that realm where the pen
of the First Intellect fell,
and to surpass their collective contributions
and leave them in her wake to fade away
    into extracanonical obscurity.

IX

We knew nothing about the Vast Earth
    of Gāiā at that point in our wayfaring—
that realm of cosmic imagination,
    that primordial cradle wherein
the sum of knowable things
    exists, and where the unknown
makes itself known by volition—

that locus within and without,
accessible to the trained third eye
    alone, where the distinct natures
of the corporeal and the subtle
    act as a blockade to the blind novice
with ambitions of free and easy access
    to both modalities of material being.

≈≈≈≈≈≈≈≈

Our sojourn at Ḥarak was emphasized
    by our complete lack of understanding
in the ways of alchemy and gnosis
    and by the fact that, though we walked
barefoot, the soles of our supple feet
    were clean—untouched by wet
        mica-speckled Vast Earth mud.

And yet, I couldn't say at the time
    with any modicum of confidence,
having observed her capacities,
    that Māyā—vicegerent to the pillars
of her discipline—had never been.

So much fruit from such a sapling
    defied the infallible laws of nature.

X

Now my being screams
    'And what about Sākina?

As you laid in shackles
    in a pitch-dark prison,
a pulp of broken bones,
    did she not place your head
on her lap and give you

cool, clean water to drink
and comfort you through
    the night, and weep for you
when praetors dragged you
    to the arena to be devoured?

And when *deus ex machina*
    interceded on your behalf
and delivered you at last
    from the mortal jaws of lions,
did she not untether you
    from the bloodied stake
then cover your nakedness
    and carry you out of the pit
through the rioting mob
    and in the night lead you
to safety beyond the gates
    of Heliopolis, and nurse you
on the banks of the East River
    as we journeyed to Ḥarak?

And did she not deprive herself
    when she offered her share
of bread to you unthinkingly
    as your broken body recovered
      from its devastating injuries?'

    Thus, my outraged soul
      chastised me.

    Truly the gentlest and kindest beings
to have every walked the earth
    would've seemed crude by comparison
to Sākina the Heliopolite, daughter
    of Umm Warda the Qumrānite.

A. A. Telmesani

Hers is verily a house of high esteem
    inestimable in wealth and station.

≈≈≈≈≈≈≈≈

From the day she entered this world,
    she was bedecked in gold
and purple silks, and ate and drank
    from fine silver and earthenware
imported from lands as far as the Seas
        of Kawthar in the East
    to the land of the Hittites
            in the West.

She is, in fact, the heiress of a vast fortune
    accumulated over generations by virtue
of a trading company whose caravans
    have for centuries traversed every route
and whose branded goods are utilized
    throughout and beyond the Zāgra Valley.

Should she ever desire a career
    as a nomarch, high priestess,
foreign emissary, or some other esteemed,
    exclusive title that she may desire,
that path is perennially available to her—
    a Qumrānite—and to no other woman

for her kin's proximity to imperial power
    is not only tangible, but historical.

The house of Qumrān has served
    Paterōns and Materōns of yore
for innumerable generations
    and has deftly navigated the snares
of regime changes and cyclical
        sectarian uprisings,

emphasizing the ancient axiom

that wealth weathers shifting tides
    and is impervious to erosion.

    And yet the quiet fire burning
        in her yearned for a reward
    of a higher ontology,
        beyond what is possible
    in the realm of corporeality
        and prime matter.

Like the flora and fauna, she too
was susceptible to the alchemic
transmutations that take place
when the Names and Formulæ
are recited aloud and recognized.

≈≈≈≈≈≈≈≈

All embodied entities in Nature
    have the capacity to recognize
the primordial Monadic language
    first spoken when Aleph issued
the command for the release
    of the Letters from their mansions
in the chaos of the Great Becoming.

    It is the fallible human being
that rapidly forgets this language
    as soon as they enter this world.

Yet there are those like Sākina
    who never lose their capacity
to recognize the primordial language
    and who are profoundly affected by it.

And, so, hearing Yāsīn and Huthayfa
    exchange recitations smote her,
and she fell into the ocean of gnosis
        and drowned.

        Her conversion,
    like that of each novitiate,
        was absolute.

≈≈≈≈≈≈≈≈

Already, she seemed to have mastered
    the art of sukūn and demonstrated
a high degree of restraint and a resilience
    to the vicissitudes she faced
in this world of codified patriarchy
    that has become a defining reality
        for Zāgran women.

Her purity of heart and wide intellect,
    fostered by tutors who taught her
the sacred traditions and sciences,
    were matched only by her rare beauty
that caused the heads of men
    and women, alike and equally,
to turn in vain attempt
    at reading the strangely perfect
contours of her features
    with an obsessive compulsion
driven by their yearning souls
        starved of ideal
    and archetypal Beauty.

Did not the Real in Her book
    proclaim that She is beautiful
and that She loves Beauty
    in all Its wondrous forms?

Truly, She is the origin of all forms,
    and so, each form is a courier
that glorifies Her—their Fashioner—
    who fashioned them
 in the Great Becoming
    of Her wondrous Names
        and Qualities.

    And it was Her breath that breathed
them into existence and assigned
    each form its own appropriate station.

    And yet, among all the divine stations
in the upraised heavenly hierarchies,
    the station of Sākina eternally resides
among the most beautiful of created things.

    But it was her mystical perspicacity—
so immediately evident—that inspired
    and propelled her well ahead in wayfaring.

I told her then that she would be
    one of the great axial saints
of our epoch and a guiding light
    to those lost in the turbulent sea
of materialism and spiritual dormancy.
    I've since been resoundingly vindicated.

≈≈≈≈≈≈≈≈

Glorious are the signs of an axial saint!
    In the rite of ablution, the cleansing
waters speak to Sākina in a unique
    dialect she alone can decipher,
and are made pure by her touch.

    In the clarity and correctness
of her Cylopiadic recitations,

had the blind ḥāfiẓ Ṣamaḍyān
himself lived to hear her recite
   from the revealed tablets,
he would have prostrated
   on bended knee before her,
kissed her feet and wept,
   humbled and humiliated
before ceding his mantle,
   and affirming her esteemed rank
as the new shaykḫa and ḥāfiẓa
   of the mujawwad and murattal,
and the seven styles of recitation
   from the seven regions of the Zāgra.

≈≈≈≈≈≈≈≈

In the act of receiving the music
   of the celestial spheres,
the orbs and astral bodies sing for her
   and exist for the sake of her.

Every note of natural harmony
   rung by the sublunar bodies
traversing the æthereal ocean
   by the will of the Unmoved Mover
that Faythāġhūrs first identified
   and arranged, were all annunciations
of the philosopher's imminent inheritor.

Her devotion to learning by heart
   the muwashshaḥ, zajal and ode
traditions of ancient Zāgran verse,
   coupled with a mnemonic capacity
to achieve such an impossible feat,
   places Sākina in her own category
and will one day ensure her status

as the custodian of Zāgran music.

And yet, these deeds and capacities
    still pale in comparison
to the profound fullness
    of her mellifluent voice—
richer and sweeter than milk and honey
    from Firdaws' fabled streams.

The estate in which she was raised from birth
    teemed with singing slave girls
plucked from the oasis palaces of Sayf Shīn,
    captured and brought back
from campaigns in Gālibūr
    against the insurrectionist
        badawī tribes.

It is said that the singing girls of Sayf Shīn
    were taught directly by the Shaṭyā clan
of jinn who have inhabited the sacred oasis
    since Gāiā's fated death in the Vast Earth.

From before she could remember,
    Sākina was lulled by the seductive
music and poetry of these slave girls
    from Sayf Shīn, and from an early age,
she learned their ways, their style of singing,
    their musical modes and their own canon
of strophic poetry that lamented a homeland
        rent asunder by the Hittites
          in the Centurial War.

Their songs live on through Sākina
    and in the hearts and souls
of those fortunate enough to hear her
    and be slain by her
devastatingly beautiful renditions.

This canon came with her
   to the monastery at Ḥarak
and became a contagion
   that struck every inhabitant,
evident in their chronic
   symptoms of perpetual singing
      and feelings
   of effervescent glee.

Kāi, Huthayfa and I sat in the grove
   to listen to Sākina sing one day
as she tended to the fig trees
   and were transported to a rare
and forbidden heavenly station
   without a proper guide other than
the lilting gossamer-winged melodies
   upon which we glided so carefree.

Amid his blissful trance, the idea
   came to Kāi to build a qānūn
of splendid red cedar
   that he could harvest
from the foothills of the Ṭāʾifā
   Plateau near the city of Ṣāḍḍ–
one that would match Sākina's
   sublime singing of folk songs.

   When he relayed his idea to us,
we were naturally overjoyed,
   and so, the next day we descended
from the plateau and located an abundance
   of old-growth red cedar, silver spruce
      and acacia trees.

      We felled one of each,
and over the course of a few days split
   and transported the timber

up to the monastery.

From these raw materials, Kāi fashioned
    the most ornate pair of instruments
I had ever seen, comprising a stunning
    qānūn and a magnificent ʿoud
that combined all three woods.

As was his signature and singular obsession,
    each instrument was neatly engraved
with the sacred Names and Qualities
    rendered in exquisite calligraphy,
then stained and accented with dyes
    of crushed indigo and wild berries.

Kāi presented his new creations
    to Sākina and was elated to learn
that she had been taught
    to play both instruments
        by the singing girls
            of Sayf Shīn.

He expressed a desire to learn
    how to play the ʿoud,
and Huthayfa the qānūn.
    And so, the following day
Sākina proceeded to share with them
    the secrets of the singing girls
of Sayf Shīn—of their ancient modes,
    their obscure intervallic systems,
and of the sacred geometry
    of Faythāghūrs' harmonic scales.

Soon thereafter, Kāi and Huthayfa
    permeated the æther in and around
the Ḥarak monastery with the music
    of the spheres and the songs of Sayf Shīn,

and in the fig grove the banyans
    sighed with delight at the sound
of their instruments and voices
    in perfect harmony that elevated
the hauntingly enchanting ballads
    that slew all partisans—of clay,
of smokeless fire, and other entities
    of lower ontological status within
the Fashioner's preternatural hierarchy.

        XI

In the spring of the second year
of our sojourn at the monastery,
on the third day of Shawwāl,
we witnessed an extraordinary
astral portent blaze across
the vast empyrean above Ḥarak
that burned candescent green
and set alight the evening sky
such that night turned to day

    before
            splitting
                    apart

    and disintegrating
        over a Zāgra Valley
            deep in slumber.

Yāsīn heeded this astral portent
    and within hours we were gone,
bound to roam the Zāgra Valley
    for some thirty years and seven
moving among her villages
    and towns and city-states,

tending to her communities
    as we tended our own fig-grove—
with a deep sense of reverence
    and an overflow of compassion.

We were to fulfill our purpose
    on this earth without trepidation
and with utter disregard
    for our own personal well-being
that others may live
      and prosper.

XII

It is better for the wanderer to mimic
    the movements of the celestial bodies,
for they occupy the superior degree
    and course across the empyrean
unburdened by material matters
    through the will of the Unmoved Mover,
the First Cause, the Benignant Master
    through whom creation ever blooms.